International Economic Sanctions

International Economic Sanctions

The Cases of Cuba, Israel, and Rhodesia

Donald L. Losman

UNIVERSITY OF NEW MEXICO PRESS

Albuquerque

Library of Congress Cataloging in Publication Data

Losman, Donald L.
    International economic sanctions

    Bibliography: p. 152
    Includes index.
    1. Boycott—Case studies. 2. Commercial policy—
Case studies. 3. International economic relations—
Case studies. 4. Sanctions (International law)—
Case studies. I. Title.
HF1416.L67   382'.3   78-21429
ISBN 0-8263-0500-8

Manufactured in the United States of America.
Library of Congress Catalog Card Number 78-21429
International Standard Book Number 0-8263-0500-8
First Edition.

Chapter 4 is an expanded version of Donald L. Losman, "The Arab
Boycott of Israel," *International Journal of Middle East Studies*,
April 1972. Published by Cambridge University Press. Reprinted by
permission.

To
Maureen

Acknowledgments

The research and writing associated with this endeavor reflect the influence, assistance, inspiration, and support of many people. Although only one name appears on the title page, a complete list of those who assisted, either directly or indirectly, would be impossible to compile. Consequently, the listing below is quite restricted. To all those named as well as those not mentioned, my heartfelt thanks. Professors Ralph Blodgett, Irving Goffman, and Robert Bradbury were inspiring and influential teachers. All were members of my doctoral supervisory committee, the latter being chairman. Shirley Cook, Judy Crain, Toney Coulter, and Latricia White rendered invaluable typing assistance. Deirdre Mahr and Michael Mahr helped with proofreading. A very special thanks is due Dwight D. Vines, president of Northeast Louisiana University, and his wife, Jean. Dr. Vines, formerly dean of the College of Business Administration, assisted in arranging release time. Even more important, both have been very good friends, have been wonderful to me and my children, and hold a very special place in my heart. My wife, Maureen, has contributed to this work through her moral support, understanding, and encouragement. Her impact upon my life and the completion of this book is incalculable.

Contents

Tables

Preface

The terms *economic sanctions* and *international boycotts* have little concrete meaning to most Americans. The average citizen, when pressed for a response, generally recognizes that they pertain to policies of refusing to buy, sell, or trade with some other nation as a punishment for some offending action or policy. In most other trading nations these terms conjure up visions of states of siege, smuggling, and suppressed or imminent hostilities. Virtue seems always to be clearly on one side; villainy, on the other. Yet beyond these generalizations, there is very little knowledge concerning how international sanctions work in practice, how effective they are, who is actually harmed by them, or how useful they are as a political tool. Indeed, judging from official statements, ignorance tends to prevail even at the highest policy levels.

The above questions are addressed in this book, emphasizing the costs upon target economies, but including the effects upon the boycotting states and third-party nations as well. Three specific embargoes are investigated: the United States boycott of Cuba, begun in 1960; the Arab boycott of Israel, which was initiated even before the Jewish state's legal creation in 1948; and the economic sanctions against Rhodesia, initially implemented by Great Britain in late 1965 and later joined by the United Nations.

Americans are most familiar with local boycotts or quasi-collective ones that operate without governmental involvement. These include efforts by various labor groups to discourage the purchase of particular domestically produced items or foreign goods and the boycotts of merchants so frequent during the civil rights struggles of the 1960s. These forms of sanctions are not covered in this study, which deals only with international boycotts implemented as an act of foreign policy by the participating nations.

I first became interested in this general topic when studying foreign trade as an undergraduate student in the early 1960s. Conversations with Cuban refugees were quite enlightening and frequently at variance with the published press releases. The Arab boycott of Israel also caught my attention. Both these embargoes were in stark contrast to the prevailing rhetoric, which favored increased world trade. The implementation of sanctions against Rhodesia in 1965 added to this list of exceptional situations. The Rhodesian sanctions were unique by virtue of the number of nations involved. These three boycotts were the topic of my doctoral dissertation at the University of Florida. This book is an outgrowth and updating of that research.

The reader will not require prior training in economics or international trade theory to grasp the argument of this book, although such knowledge is obviously advantageous. Some historical background is provided, as well as relevant analytical tools. While the history of economic thought is rich with trade theory and empirical studies showing the benefits and impacts of trade, there is little of equivalence that examines involuntary withdrawals from trade. One contribution of this work is the adaptation of traditional trade theory to such atypical situations. A second is the analysis and empirical findings. Although there is no dearth of scholarship concerning the legal and political aspects of these embargoes, almost all existing studies—apart from quoting the outcries of national leaders and enumerating a few trade statistics—deal with the economic aspects only peripherally. (An exception to this involved several careful Rhodesian studies undertaken by British scholars in the 1960s. These, however, were based upon unofficial trade estimates and data extrapolation and are now dated.) This void in economic literature is redressed in this book.

Some economists may fault this effort for its lack of technical rigor. This was by design. The book is not primarily directed to economists but rather to a broad spectrum of social scientists in the hope that they, as well as policy makers and the average citizen, will become more fully aware of the nature and impact of boycotts and of what can and should be expected from them. Both the political basis and historical importance of sanctions demand a broad audience.

The findings presented are quite relevant to current international issues and relations. Comprehensive United Nations sanctions against South Africa have repeatedly been discussed in various U.N. bodies for over a decade, and they have again been recommended and are receiving greater support than ever before.

Using sanctions to counter a second Arab oil embargo is another proposal that has appeared in the U.S. press and has been raised in some congressional hearings. Further, in the near future it is possible that the embargoes discussed here may end. An understanding of the economic impact that sanctions have had will facilitate resumption of normal relations.

I found the research involved in this effort to be exciting, stimulating, and enlightening. It is my hope that the reader will find it as worthwhile to read as I found it to write.

Donald L. Losman
U.S. Army War College

1

Introduction and History

Economic sanctions are penalties inflicted upon one or more states by one or more others, generally to coerce the target nation(s) to comply with certain norms that the boycott initiators deem proper or necessary. Sanctions may take the form of a refusal to export to the target nations, to import from it, or both. In addition, capital flows, wealth held in the boycotting states, and movements of people, both tourist and others, may be interfered with or restricted.

Three specific embargoes are investigated in this study of economic impacts of international economic sanctions: the United States boycott of Cuba; the Arab boycott of Israel; and the economic sanctions against Rhodesia. Boycotts are essentially political acts, representing instruments of foreign policy by which one state tries to bring about a change in the domestic or foreign policies of another. They are, then, a form of nonmilitary coercion that uses economic weapons to inflict hardship for the purpose of achieving certain ends.

Boycotts may have varying degrees of economic and political effectiveness. Economic effectiveness refers to the volume of pecuniary damage or disruption inflicted, while political effectiveness refers to the degree that desired changes, if any, are undertaken by the target state. A boycott may be deemed successful if it induces the target state to comply with the wishes of the boycotting nations. Generally, one would expect that to be successful, a boycott must be effective—it must impart economic hardship. Having (presumably) had no success through diplomatic pressures and wishing to avoid resort to arms, nations initiate sanctions hoping to cause sufficient economic damage to force policy (or government) change in the target country. Boycotts,

1

however, may be highly effective without necessarily being successful.

Boycotts may be classified according to the number of nations imposing them and the range of commodities covered. If imposed by only one nation, they are unilateral, as was the case initially in the Cuban and Rhodesian situations. Multilateral boycotts include the Arab boycott of Israel and the boycott of Cuba after Latin American nations joined with the United States. Current sanctions against Rhodesia may be regarded as universal, since most of the world community (with some important exceptions) is participating in accordance with U.N. resolutions. A general embargo proscribes any and all trade relations (with the possible exception of those directly related to humanitarian needs), while selective sanctions cover only a limited number of commodities. League of Nations sanctions against Mussolini's Italy are a classic example of the latter. Ironically, although the embargo was imposed to halt the Italian invasion of Ethiopia, it included neither coal nor oil, two items essential to a war economy. More recent examples include the initial boycotts against Cuba and Rhodesia, which were limited to only one item (sugar and tobacco respectively).

The enforced economic isolation of a nation has long been recognized as significant in military warfare. Naval blockades were used with success during the European wars of the eighteenth and nineteenth centuries.[1] On the other hand, the tradition of boycotting[2] has occupied a minor role historically. An early example of a boycott during the American colonial period occurred when many colonists refused to purchase certain British goods as a political protest. Later, the Jefferson administration implemented an official embargo against Britain. Charles Remer enumerates at least nine separate boycotts by Chinese nationals against the products and trade activities of other nations in the first three decades of the twentieth century, and he suggests that there probably have been more.[3] In addition, economic sanctions as a coercive devise to be used in lieu of military maneuvers were written explicitly into the Covenant of the League of Nations earlier in this century. Finally, Article 41 of the United Nations Charter allows the possibility of trade embargoes.

The origins of the term *boycott* are described in *Captain Boycott,* a book written in 1880 by an Irish author, Philip Rooney. During the nineteenth century absentee English landlords controlled much property in Ireland and demanded exorbitant rents from the tenant farmers. Captain Charles Boycott was an agent to collect these rents for one of the absentee owners. He refused to accept the farmers' payments, declaring them insufficient, and evicted many tenants. The community retaliated with a policy of total isolation, both economic and social, against the rent collector. Despite several measures, such as recruiting imported labor, Boycott could not withstand his total isolation. In the end he was forced to return to England.

"The natural starting point in any study of economic sanctions is . . . Article 16 of the League Covenant."[4] The essence of the article was that in certain circumstances the members of the League of Nations were to cease all economic intercourse with a country committing aggression. These sanctions were obligatory and were intended to prevent aggression in advance or to make it doubly difficult once begun. Concerning their potential usefulness, the report by the Committee of Economic Sanctions optimistically stated:

> The great advantage of economic sanctions is that on [the] one hand they can be very potent, while on the other hand, they do not involve that resort to force and violence which is repugnant to our objective of peace. If any machinery can be set up to ensure that nations comply with their covenant to renounce war, such machinery must be sought primarily in the economic sphere.[5]

Unfortunately, implementation of Article 16 was difficult because of inherent weaknesses capable of frustrating its purpose. First, Article 16 demanded complete and total nonintercourse, a measure whose effects would be felt unevenly by the boycotting states. Some of these might be so economically tied to the aggressor nation that complete nonintercourse would be an act of economic suicide. This possible consequence, therefore, acted as a deterrent to the article's being invoked and as a practical obstacle to full compliance, if it were.

In addition, for humanitarian reasons the actual implementation of a total embargo—one embracing foods, medicines, and other commodities vital to the civilian population and those unconnected with military aggression—would probably not be acceptable to world opinion. As one writer suggested: "For effectiveness, and for moral standing, a really successful food embargo ranks well in advance of torpedoing hospital ships and is somewhere near the class of gassing maternity hospitals."[6] These stern measures, however, have been defended on the basis of their preventive capabilities. Such a "complete and immediate severance of all relations may appear at first . . . to be too severe. . . . But it should not be forgotten that the aggressor is fully aware in advance of the consequences of its act."[7] Thus it is apparent that for economic sanctions to be successful in preventing aggression, the aggressor state must feel certain that a boycott will actually be implemented and that it will be total rather than partial. Since full economic sanctions were never invoked under the League, the hypothesis that world opinion would not tolerate a complete embargo was not tested.

There were additional and more significant weaknesses of League sanctions, each of a very practical nature. Each member state had the right to decide for itself whether or not conditions had come to the point where League sanctions could be invoked. The strong likelihood of differing interpretations in the event of such a situation would probably have resulted in partial and isolated attempts at boycotts, all insufficient to stop aggression. Another weakness was the potential of embargoes to harm the enforcing states. Finally, the fact that neither the Soviet Union nor the United States was a League member opened the possibility for frustrating League boycotts through trade with these two nations.

The League of Nations did invoke Article 16 in two instances. On October 4, 1935, Mussolini's forces invaded Ethiopia after a skirmish between Italian and Ethopian forces in an isolated but politically contested oasis in Eritrea. This action brought a storm of protest from the other nations of Europe. The League Council met and eventually declared that economic and financial sanctions be invoked.[8]

These sanctions proved unsuccessful both in preventing hostilities and in bringing the aggression to a quick end. Mussolini had been telling the Italian people for years that they were surrounded by other nations bent on destroying Italy. The embargo provided justification for an austerity campaign in which food and clothing were carefully rationed. Thus, domestic economizing partially offset the boycott's effect. In addition, the actual embargo was not total, with perhaps the two most vital items to a war machine, oil and coal, being exempted. The facts, however, that both England and France were large producers of coal, that British colonies produced oil, and that both countries were Council members, makes the Council's decision more readily explainable. The boycott's uneven effect upon the implementing nations was also brought to light by Britain's refusal to deny Italy access to the Suez Canal, Britain having a good deal to lose financially by such a move. There were, of course, other important considerations that were noneconomic in character.

Finally, other nations defied the sanctions. Germany seemed especially eager to provide supplies to Italy, probably because Italian involvement in an African war meant that less attention was given to Austria, which thus became easier prey for Germany. Russia, too, carried on substantial trade with the Italians. Thus, because of its open relations with Germany, Russia, and the United States, and its barely camouflaged trade with France and England, Italy was able to defy successfully League economic sanctions.

In September 1938, at the prodding of China's representative, sanctions were imposed on Japan for bombing Chinese cities. By this time, however, the weakness and inability of League boycott efforts were so patent that the sanctions were almost immediately rescinded, an action taken after the British suggested that the League merely express its sympathy to China and drop the entire matter. The ineffectiveness of League actions in dealing with Italy and Japan contributed to the collapse of Woodrow Wilson's dream of international peace, although it may have been destined to fail almost from its inception.

Several other twentieth century examples of international sanctions merit mention. Between 1939 and 1945 the Allied powers implemented a number of effective embargoes. In the postwar period, under the Export Control Act, the United States for years abstained from trade with several Communist nations. In 1960 the Organization of American States invoked sanctions upon the Dominican Republic for alleged aggression and intervention in Venezuela. Further, the use of sanctions has not been limited to the non-Communist world. In 1948 the Soviet Union and its satellites expelled Yugoslavia from CEMA (the Council on Mutual Economic Aid, a socialist-bloc regional trade and planning association) and suspended all trade and payments with that country. A similar although less pervasive action was taken against Albania in 1961 when the latter was accused of "defecting" to the Chinese Communists. Finally, the United Nations charter expressly provides for the use of economic measures to maintain or restore the peace, with U.N. provisions improving upon weaknesses in League of Nations procedures. Several other differences make the U.N.'s use of sanctions, at least on paper, more likely to succeed than that of the League. In particular, the freedom of action "enjoyed by League members in taking, or not taking, enforcement action . . . disappears in the United Nations system. . . ."[9]

2

Trade Theory, Boycott Vulnerability, and Costs

The gains and benefits of international trade have occupied a position of importance in both the economic policy of governments and the theory of academicians for over two hundred years. While exceptions have been occasionally noted, the advantages accruing from the international division of labor and specialization are recognized to have an expansionary effect upon aggregate world product as well as upon the national dividend of each voluntarily participating nation. Over the years, trade theory has been refined and sophisticated, from absolute advantage to comparative advantage, from two-country, two-commodity trade to multilateral, multiproduct exchange. Emphasis has shifted from the older concern with the direction of trade to a more recent preoccupation with the volume of international transactions. The essense of the theory, however, is basically unchanged.[1] A nation can avail itself of greater amounts of goods and services than it could produce by itself by means of specialization and international trade. In short, a "country's access to a foreign market has a real income effect that is essentially the same as if there had been an outward shift in its production frontier."[2]

The benefits from trade basically derive from differences in comparative costs, which result from a variety of causes, chief among them being unequal factor endowments, differing technologies, and diverse utility and preference functions. The gains from trade will tend to be greater: (1) the more domestic opportunity costs differ from corresponding production costs in other countries; (2) the smaller any one country is, relative to its trading partners; (3) the easier it is to gain access to foreign markets; and, finally, (4) the smaller the slope of the cost gradients both at home and abroad.[3]

7

These benefits merit explanation. Trade is beneficial only to the extent that domestic cost ratios differ from the corresponding foreign ratios, and the greater the difference between the two, the greater the scope for gain by means of specialization and trade. It will be economic for a nation to import those goods for which it possesses a comparative disadvantage and export those for which it has a comparative advantage. To the extent that prices accurately reflect relative scarcities, the greater the difference between world-wide prices and a country's own prices in the absence of trade, the more potential benefit.[4] The same reasoning suggests that trade tends to dissipate when the domestic price ratios (opportunity costs) become equal to foreign ratios. In short, as domestic and foreign prices are brought into line, the incremental gains from trade diminish. Cost ratios are not usually constant but tend to vary with the volume of production and degree of specialization. Therefore the more rapidly both domestic and foreign ratios tend to change (the steeper the cost gradients), the sooner they equalize. Conversely, the more slowly they come together, the greater the scope for advantageous exchange.

It can also be seen that the size of a nation relates to its benefits from trade. This is true because large nations tend to have greater populations and other resources that allow considerable specialization within their own borders. Small nations, on the other hand, cannot carry the division of labor to such a great extent internally; hence, the smaller the nation, the greater the potential benefits from international trade. Accordingly, a large resource base has a trade-reducing effect. Nevertheless, the volume of trade tends to be greatest among the larger, industrially advanced nations rather than among the less-developed countries or between advanced states and economically poor ones. This is true because the trade-reducing effect of large size is more than offset by the income effect permitted by such size. The expansion of economic opportunities made possible by (and accompanying) growth and a large national output enhances chances for mutually advantageous exchange. Linneman's studies indicate that the volume of trade between two regions tends to be directly proportional to the national income of the areas and inversely proportional to the distance between them.[5] Finally, the easier it is to gain access to foreign markets—either through reducing natural barriers with transport improvements or selling innovations, or through reducing artificial barriers such as tariffs and quotas—the greater the sphere of gainful exchange.

There are additional benefits from unimpeded international trade that are more qualitative than the important—though often difficult to measure—advantages already introduced. Following Adam Smith's famous dictum that "the division of labor is limited by the extent of the market," it can be seen that access to foreign markets, by enlarging product demand, can allow the use of large-scale economies and new technology. Mass-production techniques would be uneconomic if an unsalable surplus were the only result. Disposal of high-volume, low-cost output by means of international as well as domestic trade has a positive income effect upon both producing and consuming nations.

Trade also serves to link markets together, thereby providing increased knowledge of conditions, qualities, and prices—all of which tend to allocate world resources more efficiently. Beyond this, diversified trade "serves as a kind of safety valve or shock absorber, allowing random economic disturbances in different places partially to offset each other."[6] Perhaps most important, trade may instill dynamism and vigor, which act as spurs to efficiency and innovation. The foreign-trade sector in the developing areas can be the starting point from which entrepreneurial abilities and related functions spread into the broader domestic economy. Moreover, the added competition from foreign producers penalizes inefficiency and stimulates innovation in all economies, advanced or developing. Last, but very important for new nations, trade tends to have a "demonstration effect" that can raise national effort, attitude, and output, by enhancing national aspirations and piquing a desire for achievement.[7]

Participation in international trade, then, has significant economic effects. Both the reallocations that would result from a static long-run equilibrium situation and the output effects of the dynamic aspects of trade result in increased real income. The necessary conditions for static long-run equilibrium under completely free international trade are twofold: in the product market, equality of prices (ignoring transport and marketing costs) of all economic goods of a given quality in all countries; and in the factor market, equality of earnings of the agents of production for supplying services of a given quality. Fulfillment of these two conditions would result in the real cost ratios in each nation being equal to each other and to the price ratios of the goods produced. Such an equilibrium would create an optimum distribution of the factors of production and a maximum world output. That the real world falls short of these conditions is an obvious truism. Because of ignorance, immobilities, rigidities, and a host of other factors—some contrived and others natural—the full benefits of international trade are never realized.

Nevertheless, from the point of view of a particular nation, imperfections in the outside world must be taken as given data. "Trade offers a country worthwhile opportunities regardless of why world-market prices differ (actually or virtually) from its own."[8] As Harrod has suggested:

> Since we are considering . . . how any particular country can, taking the conditions in the outer world as given, best utilize her resources, the question of the conformity between the foreign cost structure and the world price structure becomes irrelevant. The best that a particular country can do for herself is to make her own price structure correspond to her own cost structure and to enter into such foreign trade as is consistent with that condition and with the prevailing world price structure.[9]

This brief survey reaffirms the fact that the benefits from international trade are real and substantial. Although there exists no general agreement among economists concerning the distribution of the gains from trade, it must be assumed that in a situation of voluntary exchange all parties do receive (or expect to receive) some benefit. "The logic of this case is beyond criticism . . .,"[10] although we should not infer that all trade has historically been voluntary, and therefore, beneficial.

The static benefits from trade as well as the nature of the cost of sanctions are illustrated in Figure 1. Participation in trade moves the economy's transformation curve outward, from P_2 to P_1. Any involuntary withdrawal from trade, as may be forced by sanctions, will reduce the scope of consumption possibilities so that they coincide with domestic production possibilities, that is transformation curve P_1 is no longer attainable. Further, in the short run the economy's actual operating point will move inward due to trade-related dislocations, perhaps to points A or B. The greater the linkages of the foreign-trade sector with the general

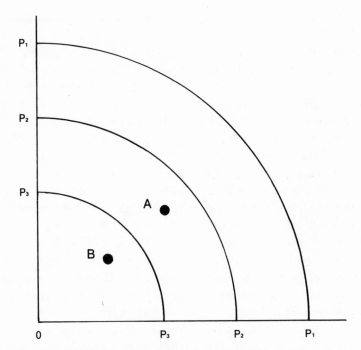

Fig. 1. Schematic representation of transformation curve

economy, the greater the unemployment and adjustment costs and the more likely it is that actual operations will move inward from the production frontier. Last, the domestic transformation curve itself may also move inward. Such movement will be designated "capital effects," and could result from either of two causes. First, some of the nation's productive wealth, if manufactured abroad, may be rendered useless or ineffective if vital spare parts cannot be obtained. Second, if former imports included intermediate goods for which domestic production is difficult or impossible, some production (and factories) may have to be abandoned. If "capital effects" are operative, production possibilities are further reduced and will shrink to curve P3.

The costs inflicted by economic sanctions may be classified as direct, indirect, foregone potential, and "capital effects." These definitions are somewhat arbitrary and areas of overlap would be found in practice; however, the classification aids analysis and these costs can, in varying degrees, be expected to prevail in almost all boycott situations.

Direct costs entail additional financial or real outlays immediately and directly related to the imposition of sanctions.

Increased transport expenses are perhaps the best example. Thus, before the creation of the state of Israel, Palestine imported certain raw materials from its Arab neighbors. In particular crude oil was brought through pipeline, a relatively inexpensive method. Since the creation of the state in 1948, oil has had to be purchased in far more distant markets, such as Venezuela and Iran, thus adding to Israel's balance-of-payments difficulties.[11] Cuba imported its petroleum from a nearby Latin American source before 1960 and most of its capital equipment came from the United States. Today, the Soviet Union and the nations of Europe are Cuba's major, and far more distant, suppliers.[12]

Another example of direct costs is the loss of traditional export revenues. Although the term "traditional" is somewhat hazy, examples are not hard to find. Cuba after 1960 lost a guaranteed sugar market (with a profitable quota premium) and a traditionally lucrative tourist industry. Tobacco's role in Rhodesia was similar to that of sugar in Cuba. It provided the chief source of Rhodesian foreign exchange until 1966 when the industry was severely damaged by the singular effectiveness of U.N. sanctions on tobacco. Unemployment in the foreign-trade sector would be still another example of direct costs to the target state.

Indirect costs derive from the many domestic dislocations and slowdowns that result from a disruption of normal foreign trade. These particularly relate to imports of intermediate products and raw materials. The adverse production effects resulting from the difficulty of substituting domestic inputs for imported ones has been termed an "import bottleneck."[13] This implies that disruptions of intermediate product imports may significantly increase costs when technical adaptability to domestic substitutes is poor or lacking. For example, if domestic sources of fuel, such as sugar, must be utilized in lieu of petroleum imports, vehicles and machinery may still be employed but with more frequent breakdowns and more rapid depreciation. Hence, in addition to the greater direct real costs of the goods, their use entails additional, indirect costs. Another example of an indirect cost is unemployment in nontrade sectors. For example, if a Rhodesian tobacco worker, unemployed because of sanctions, stops having three beers each Friday at the local tavern, the nontrade sector is adversely affected, although this sector itself is not directly vulnerable to sanctions.

When alternative foreign suppliers can be found, but the distances involved are much greater and quality of product poorer, similar problems are created. Thus, in the Cuban situation several raw materials formerly imported from the United States had to be procured from China. The trip, however, took two months and schedules were only rarely kept. This meant that some factories and men were idled by late deliveries; nonproduction in that sector in turn led to nonproduction elsewhere, and so forth. When qualitative differences in the new imports appear, similar disruptions may prevail, even when quality is not necessarily "lower." In the case of Cuba, for example, the importation of Soviet tractors and machinery caused serious problems because even though well constructed, they were built for an entirely different climate, tended to overheat quickly, and thus were subject to excessive breakdowns. Much machinery was nevertheless usable, yet very serious problems still arose because Soviet agricultural equipment was not geared to the production habits and techniques traditionally used in Cuba. Machines designed for cultivating rows of a specific width proved totally useless when Cuban plantings departed from their measurements. The outskirts of Havana have for years been littered with tons of unsuitable, Soviet-built agricultural equipment that had to be junked.

Another cost, probably best classified as an indirect one, relates to storage and warehousing expenses. In the Rhodesian situation, in order to placate the farmers politically and ease disruptions in the economy, the government purchased the tobacco crop, marketing what it could. Sanctions on tobacco have been quite effective and considerable stockpiling has occurred, requiring a commitment of resources to storage facilities.[14] Cuba has had to construct similar facilities in order to house the bulk shipments received from the U.S.S.R. Formerly, orders sent to the United States were timed according to Cuban needs and delivered in conveniently sized lots.

The "capital effects" already described may perhaps be more properly classified as an indirect cost; however, their distinctive aspects and potential importance merit separate treatment.

Foregone potential costs refer to the failure of some economic variables to grow or improve as rapidly as would otherwise have been the case. In Cuba's case, it was doubtful that the country's position in the American sugar market would have changed, but

there is little question that its tourist industry, geared to
Americans, would have continued its steady growth. With the
boycott, however, these potential foreign exchange earnings were
never realized. Similarly, although both Israel and Rhodesia have
significant tourist industries there is little doubt that these
industries would be more important in the absence of the
boycott.[15] Before 1948, tourist excursions to the entire Middle
East were offered—one could visit the Holy Land, see the
Pyramids, Damascus, Lebanon, and other places of interest in a
single visit. Today two trips are necessary; one must visit the Arab
Middle East, leave the region, and then return to visit Israel.

Certain economies on the cost side may also remain unrealized.
Rhodesia formerly had an expanding market for manufactured
items in neighboring black states. Continued growth in the scale of
the market might have made possible further production
economies. Sanctions, however, have operated to preclude
realizing this potential.

Sanctions cannot be imposed upon others without costs to the
boycotting states as well. Because trade is a two-way street, those
states severing commercial ties with another are likely to find that
they must shift to more costly or more distant suppliers, while on
the revenue side the demand for their products will be reduced. In
some instances, the costs of fully imposing sanctions may be
unbearable. This was certainly the situation in the case of Zambia,
probably Rhodesia's staunchest political adversary. Yet the
dependence by Zambia on Rhodesian products was simply too
great to allow a complete severing of trade relations. In the Arab
world, Jordan, by adhering to the boycott of Israel, denies itself a
quick and economical efficient outlet to the sea. As a rule,
however, the loss to the imposing nations is far less, since they are
economically larger and can turn to a variety of alternative
suppliers and markets. The greater the number (and economic
importance) of states imposing sanctions, the higher the costs to
the target nation, whose alternatives have been substantially
reduced.

The larger the ratio of imports and exports to national income in
the target state, the greater the disruptive effects that sanctions are
likely to cause. If import substitution is very costly (or impossible),
and if the items imported are production or consumption
necessities, a diminished rate of inflow is likely to be seriously
disruptive. This suggests that the less flexible the target state's

demand for imports, the greater the target state's vulnerability. A further consideration would be the point at which the boycotted nation's demand for imports cuts the vertical axis. The higher the intersection, the more costly the sanctions will be.

Elasticity of import demand merits some elaboration. Elasticity is a function of a variety of factors, of which the three seemingly most important are: (1) whether the goods involved are considered luxuries or necessities; (2) the availability of substitutes—domestic or foreign; and (3) the time period involved. With regard to the first factor, it makes a great deal of difference whether the products of the boycotting states are considered luxuries or necessities in the target nations. If, for example, Italy were to boycott the United States and in the process deny that country its supply of olives, the economic impact of the boycott (assuming these to be the only goods involved) would be minimal. On the other hand, if petroleum or some other item of vital importance were involved, the impact upon the target nation would be much greater.

In a similar vein, if substitute supply sources are readily available, the boycott may entail some additional transport costs but would hardly cause significant domestic dislocations. The number, nature, and ecomonic distance of the nonboycotting nations are relevant criteria in determining the availability of substitute supply sources. In addition, if import substitution is both technically and economically feasible, again the impact of the boycott will be mitigated. On the other hand, if alternate suppliers cannot be found, such as might be the situation in a truly universal boycott or as in the case of Cuba, in which alternative suppliers were not able to provide the spare parts and raw materials traditionally used, then the impact becomes more severe. In each of these situations, the greater the inelasticity of demand is for the goods of the boycotting states, the greater is the likely economic impact.

Finally, the time period involved is important. In relatively short-run periods demand tends to be inelastic. Over time, however, new processes may be discovered that lessen the necessity to import, synthetics may displace natural raw materials, and a host of other adjustments can be introduced. This suggests that boycotts tend to be most effective in the short-run when dependence upon the goods previously supplied externally is still strong, but enough time has not elapsed for successful import substitution and other adaptive measures. As an example, in Cuba the dependence upon American parts and raw materials continually lessened as Western European and Socialist-bloc capital goods, technology, and intermediate products became more fully entrenched.

When estimating the damage inflicted, it is important to isolate those costs that justifiably stem from the boycott from those caused by extraneous factors. While this is not difficult in theory, in practice it presents many problems. The very conditions that gave rise to boycotts can introduce so many changing variables that the isolation of boycott-induced costs becomes a very complex matter. For instance, Cuba unquestionably experienced declines in real output after the imposition of the American embargo.[16] These decreases, however, may have been in part the result of the exodus of trained manpower, radical institutional reorganizations, poor planning, or even sabotage. In Rhodesia's case, although real gross national income fell by roughly 3.9 percent during 1966,[17] the first full year of sanctions, could this decrease not also be attributed to prior emigration or growing racial tensions?

Conversely, is it not possible—indeed, likely in the short run—that in the face of sanctions the nation would be stimulated to greater achievements, so that under *ceteris paribus* conditions the actual declines would have been much greater than 3.9 percent? The isolation of particular impacts deriving from each factor becomes very difficult when other variables are brought into consideration. In sum, actual decreases in output may either overstate or understate the impact of sanctions alone.

It should be noted that elementary Keynesian multiplier analysis probably cannot provide even a rough estimate of the income effects of boycotts. This is true because essentially only final goods are considered when computing the ordinary foreign trade multiplier. Since the real benefits of trade derive from imports, some consideration of the importance of intermediate product imports must be taken if the impact of sanctions is to be reasonably estimated. Professor Miyazawa has demonstrated that such imports are determined by the technological needs and structure of the domestic economy.[18] He derives a multiplier that, in basic essentials, is:

$$\frac{1}{[1-(b-m_b-m_j)]},$$

where b is the marginal propensity to consume; m_b the marginal propensity to import final goods; and m_j a technologically determined propensity to import intermediate products. Spare parts, raw materials, and semifinished product imports are often vital for domestic production processes, and an enforced import cessation can be very damaging. Yet ordinary foreign trade multipliers ignore this.

A simple illustration will demonstrate the inadequacy of elementary multiplier analysis. Assume that trade is balanced prior to sanctions so that after their imposition imports and exports fall by the same amount. If the foreign trade multiplier then equaled 2, with exports falling by $10, income would tend to fall by $20. However, the reduced injection (export earnings) is offset by an equal reduction in import leakages. The money income effect is apparently neutral.[19] Yet this is too simple. The true net effects depend very much upon the nature of the goods imported, their relative role in domestic production processes, and the possibility of import substitution. If rock-and-roll records are the only items imported, domestic substitutes of some form are likely to appear. Spending on the former imports becomes channeled into the domestic spending stream. As in the example above, there is no net money income effect. On the other hand, if petroleum was the product imported and at the same time the sole source of power, completely unavailable domestically, then the situation is vitally changed. A cessation of petroleum imports will stop production over wide areas of the economy. The income loss of $20 (due to decreased exports) will not be offset by spending on domestic substitutes. Without oil a tremendous slowdown will result. Both money and real income are likely to fall by considerable amounts. The decline in money income could perhaps be prevented by government deficit spending, subsidies, and public works; however, in this example, with so vital an import lost, it would take enormous public injections that, in the face of declining output, would probably result in rampant inflation.

Professor Holzman, addressing himself to a different problem, has derived a formula that expresses the sequential process by which import sanctions disrupt domestic production.[20] His formulations confirm the research findings upon which this work is based: sanctions have the greatest potential for damage in the areas of raw material imports and intermediate goods. Their ultimate impact essentially depends upon three major variables: (1) the proportion of total national output produced by industries depending either directly or indirectly upon intermediate product imports no longer available; (2) the technological significance of imports and the ratio of the value of such goods to the value of final output in the utilizing industries; and (3) the ability to muster import susbstitutes. The latter factor, mitigating a boycott's impact, is a function of available domestic resources, their technological adaptability, and any previous accumulations of essential imports or import substitutes.

Imports are linked with the domestic production process as follows. A sanctions-induced import cessation disrupts production in the importing industry, say industry A, the extent being determined by the ratio of imports to total output and the technological "fit" of imports in the production process.[21] This disruption then affects other industries (say B and C) for which industry A is a supplier. Bottlenecks in B and C in turn spread elsewhere through this same process. The degree of disruption in each instance will again depend upon the importance of imports (or inputs derived from them) and the ability to find usable import substitutes.

Import substitution, where possible, will prevent or lessen production disruptions in the target economy. The longer sanctions are in force, the more likely it is that import substitutes will be found. It should, however, also be noted that such substitution as a rule also entails costs. As one study concluded, "import substitution may . . . spread a country's resources too thin over numerous small and inefficient enterprises, and extend to types of production ill suited to its conditions."[22] Since the kind of import substitution just described and generally studied is voluntary, while that due to sanctions is coerced and hurried, it is all the more likely that the resulting inefficiencies and increases in cost will appear sooner and be of greater magnitude.

This has certainly happened in Cuba, although it should be noted that prior accumulations of imports (because of impending tariff increases) mitigated both the production disruptions and the generalized cost increases. By late 1961, however, as inventories were depleted, severe shortages of essential materials began to appear. Production stoppages and unemployment of both men and machines on a massive scale occurred. A hurried import substitution was undertaken, with the result that real costs increased considerably and quality of output suffered significantly.

In the Rhodesian instance, production disruptions from sanctions were also mitigated by the accumulation of inventories that occurred after the threat of economic boycott was first recognized, but before the actual imposition. In addition, the structure and technology of the Rhodesian economy enabled it to withstand sanctions: it possessed considerable scope for successful import substitution. Although quality of output has also deteriorated for many products because of inexperience with new production processes, inferior raw materials, and so forth, the declines have been nowhere as serious as in Cuba and generally represent inconveniences rather than hardships.

Vulnerability to sanctions, then, tends to be greatest for nations in which foreign trade plays a major role. In addition, if foreign commerce is concentrated in one or two major exports that dominate the target economy, or is concentrated in terms of markets and suppliers, extreme vulnerability exists. The nature of imports and their role in domestic production processes is also a major variable. If the target economy is technologically tied to suppliers that impose sanctions, without suitable substitute suppliers, the economic damage can be quite severe. Finally, when the boycotting states are geographically close,[23] with trade following lines of comparative advantage, sanctions will be costlier than otherwise would be the case.

3

The Embargo of Cuba

Most developing countries, to varying degrees, have encountered the kinds of economic difficulties that contemporary Cuba has experienced, including overambitious investment efforts in the face of severe foreign exchange constraints, demographic problems, inexperienced planners, and operational difficulties in nationalized industries. Few, however, have been boycotted by their major supplier and market so that a significant restructuring of foreign trade became mandatory.[1] While innumerable studies of Cuba's economic problems have been made, most include only brief references to the "difficulties arising from the American embargo" or the problems resulting from a "severance of trade relations with the United States."[2] In the analyses of Cuba's economic measures—their successes and failures—the role of the boycott, its economic impact upon the Cuban economy, and the economic dislocations and adjustments that Cuba has been forced to undergo, have been virtually ignored.

Introduction and Background

The origins and nature of the Castro movement have been well documented and need not be detailed here.[3] What is important to recognize is that Castro's revolution was the product of instabilities long evident in Cuban society. It represented the crystallization of a revolutionary process characteristic of most of twentieth-century Cuba and earlier. Cuba's client status as well as several blunders in American policy evoked antagonism toward the United States,[4] as did the scope of American investment, however much the latter contributed to the economy.[5] American paternalism seems to have had both altruistic and selfish motivations, neither of which engendered positive feelings toward the United States. Against this background, a strident nationalism and a desire for self-improvement emerged, and it is not surprising that the yearning to come out from the shadow and tutelage of the "colossus to the North" was patently evident in the new Castro regime.

Whether Castro was or was not a Communist prior to his coming to power is a moot question. More important, the question is somewhat irrelevant since many of the subsequent political events that occurred were likely to have resulted and evoked similar responses, both internal and external, regardless of Castro's particular ideological commitments.[6]

The decaying political relationship between the United States and the Castro regime (coupled with the American suspension of the Cuban sugar quota) resulted in significantly decreased trade between the two nations during the 1959–60 period. In October 1960, the United States placed an official embargo on exports to Cuba (medical supplies and foodstuffs were formally excepted). More than 60 percent of Cuba's exports went to the American market during the 1950s, but the 1961 figure fell to less than 5 percent. With regard to imports, the United States supplied roughly 70 percent of Cuba's total in 1958 and about 68 percent in 1959; by 1961, however, the figure had fallen to less than 4 percent. Since 1962 trade between the two nations (limited to vital medical supplies or purchases by international organizations) has been almost nil.[7] The American Export Control Act is legally binding upon Americans whether they reside in the United States or abroad; it also applies to overseas American subsidiaries if they have American officers or directors. Moreover, foreign businessmen will lose import privileges if any American goods purchased are willfully reexported to Cuba. Every possible effort has been made to isolate Cuba economically. Naturally, the other nations of the Western Hemisphere are among the third-party countries to which American efforts have been directed. Further, in 1964, the Organization of American States (O.A.S.) officially suspended all trade and shipping with Cuba due both to American pressure and to political tensions between the Castro regime and several Latin American states.

The Structure of Foreign Trade and Payments

Table 1 represents the geographical distribution of Cuba's foreign trade for the ten years immediately preceding the Castro regime. Dominance of the United States as the leading trade partner is immediately evident. For the entire period the table indicates that 79.8 percent of Cuba's imports came from the United States and Latin America, with these areas absorbing 65.2 percent of Cuba's exports. In short, the sanctions were applied by the most important trade partners and necessitated restructuring Cuban trade patterns. The table also indicates that Western Europe constituted the major non-Western Hemisphere trade partner, absorbing more than one-fifth of Cuba's exports (essentially sugar) and supplying 11.6 percent of Cuban imports. Canada was the next most significant trade partner, but hardly an important one, while commercial relations with Communist nations, Japan, and others were quite small. It is interesting that while imports from the socialist bloc accounted for less than one-half of 1 percent of Cuba's total, exports to the bloc, although small absolutely, were four

TABLE 1
Geographical Distribution of Cuba's Foreign Trade, 1949—58
(in thousands of dollars)

Trade Partner	Average Annual Imports		Average Annual Exports	
	Amount	%	Amount	%
United States of America[a]	$450,368	75.4	$415,469	62.5
Canada	14,333	2.4	9,101	1.4
Latin America	26,549	4.4	17,896	2.7
Europe (non-Communist)[b]	69,708	11.6	141,109	21.4
Soviet Union	3	—	10,826	1.5
Communist Europe[c]	1,361	0.2	1,417	0.2
Japan	2,536	0.4	32,566	4.9
Communist China[d]	52	0.1	1,079	0.2
Other countries	32,759	5.5	34,636	5.2
	$597,669	100.0	$664,099	100.0

[a]Not including Puerto Rico

[b]Europe, excluding the Soviet Union and countries included in note c.

[c]Albania, Bulgaria, Czechoslovakia (90 percent of imports), Estonia, Hungary, Latvia, Lithuania, Poland, Rumania, East Germany, and Yugoslavia.

[d]Includes Manchuria

Source: Cuban Economic Research Project, *Stages and Problems of Industrial Development in Cuba* (Coral Gables, Fla.: University of Miami Press, 1965), p. 183.

times the value of imports. This indicates that the proceeds of sales to bloc nations were used mainly to purchase Western Hemisphere or Western European goods rather than Communist ones.

Table 2 shows the commodity composition of imports in 1954, a pre-Castro year considered typical. Producer goods account for almost 54 percent of the total. The largest single category of imports is foodstuffs (28.6 percent), followed closely by raw materials (26.6 percent), the latter group accounting for roughly half of the producer goods imports.

Given these traditional trade patterns, it seems logical to suppose that the trade adjustments necessitated by the embargo would have resulted in an enormous increase in Cuban trade with Western nonboycotting nations. Table 1 indicates that these states supplied almost 20 percent of Cuba's imports over the 1949–58 period. It is reasonable to conclude that Cuba's import needs

TABLE 2
Composition and Value of Cuban Imports, 1954
(in millions of U.S. dollars)

Item	Value	%
Consumer goods:		
Clothing	1.5	.3
Household articles	34.7	7.1
Automobiles	25.6	5.2
Luxury	2.1	.4
Foodstuffs	139.9	28.6
Medicines	11.1	2.2
Tobacco	1.1	.2
Beverages	6.2	1.2
Other	4.2	.8
Total Consumer Goods	226.4	46.0
Producer goods:		
Sugar industry	2.6	.5
Other industries	51.2	10.4
Agriculture	13.4	2.7
Transport	12.8	2.6
Construction goods	17.7	3.6
Fuels	33.7	6.9
Raw materials	130.1	26.6
Total Producer Goods	261.5	53.3
Total, Consumer and Producer Goods	487.9	100.0 [a]

[a]Total does not exactly equal 100 due to rounding.

Source: Adapted from U.S. Department of Commerce, Bureau of Foreign Commerce, *Investment in Cuba* (July 1956), p. 140.

would have been met by supply sources relatively close, thus minimizing transport costs. Accordingly, the nations of Western Europe appear as logical suppliers rather than the more distant countries of Eastern Europe and the Soviet Union. Canada, too, must be included as a natural source of supply in lieu of the United States. In the Far East, Japan is a much more likely supplier than Communist China. These conclusions are reinforced by the aforementioned historical trade patterns, ties far broader and older than the very meager economic relations that existed between Cuba and the socialist bloc. A third factor in this consideration of adjusted trade patterns is the fact that consumption patterns and technological needs in Cuba again all point to expanded trade with Western nations and Japan. At the technical level, tractors and machinery from Canada, Britain, and Spain were more likely to suit Cuba's industrial and technological needs. Finally, in terms of simple communications, Russian and the Eastern European languages are alien to Cuba, whereas English, already widely used on the island, and Spanish are both readily useable in most of the West. In short, in the absence of special circumstances, Cuba's trade patterns would naturally have gravitated toward a major expansion with the nonboycotting Western nations.

The anticipated expansions did not materialize, however, as is indicated in Table 3. The socialist bloc became Cuba's dominant trade partner, supplying 79.8 percent of Cuba's imports by 1966 and absorbing 81.4 percent of Cuban exports in that same year. Imports from nonboycotting Western nations did increase—to 30 percent of Cuba's total in 1961—but over the 1961–67 period averaged no more than 25 percent, not a major change from the figure of earlier years. Over this same period, Cuban exports to these nations averaged roughly one-fourth of the export totals.

These statistics raise an obvious question: Why was trade not diverted to the "second-best" trade partners after the traditional ones were lost? What factors contributed to the bulk of trade being diverted to the least likely group of nations? The answer to these questions is found essentially in Cuba's inability to accumulate hard currency earnings. This deficiency was in very large measure the result of the boycott and its pervasive impacts. For ideological reasons, of course, the socialist bloc may have appeared as a more desirable trade partner; however, the economics of the situation (ignoring, at this juncture, socialist aid) clearly dictated a trade expansion with Western nonboycotting states.

TABLE 3

Cuban Foreign Trade, 1959—67

(in millions of dollars)

	1959	% of Total	1960	% of Total	1961	% of Total	1962	% of Total	1963	% of Total	1964	% of Total	1965	% of Total	1966	% of Total	1967	% of Total
Exports to:																		
Nonbloc nations[a]	$623.9	97.8	$468.3	75.8	$166.6	26.7	$93.9	18.0	$117.3	32.6	$291.4	40.8	$148.0	21.6	$110.0	18.6	$134.0	18.8
Socialist nations	13.9	2.2	149.9	24.2	458.3	73.3	426.8	82.0	366.5	67.4	422.4	59.2	538.0	78.4	482.0	81.4	581.0	81.2
Total	$637.8	100.0	$618.2	100.0	$624.9	100.0	$520.7	100.0	$543.8	100.0	$713.8	100.0	$686.0	100.0	$592.0	100.0	$715.0	100.0
Imports from:																		
Nonbloc nations[b]	$673.0	99.7	$518.7	81.3	$211.0	30.0	$130.5	17.2	$163.6	23.2	$331.6	32.5	$208.0	24.0	$187.0	20.2	$207.0	20.9
Socialist nations	1.8	0.3	119.2	18.7	491.6	70.0	629.0	82.8	703.7	76.8	687.2	67.5	657.0	76.0	739.0	79.8	783.0	79.1
Total	$674.8	100.0	$637.9	100.0	$702.6	100.0	$759.5	100.0	$867.3	100.0	$1,018.8	100.0	$865.0	100.0	$926.0	100.0	$990.0	100.0
Trade Balance																		
With nonbloc nations	−50.9		−50.4		−44.4		−36.6		13.7		− 40.2		− 60.0		− 77.0[c]		− 73.0[d]	
With socialist nations	12.1		30.7		−33.3		−202.2		−337.2		−264.8		−119.0		−257.0		−202.0	
Overall	−38.8		−19.7		−77.7		−238.8		−323.5		−305.0		−179.0		−334.0[c]		−275.0[d]	

a U.S. included through 1962.

b U.S. included through 1963.

c Official Cuba data from JUCEPLAN differ from IMF data, the Cuban figure being $99 million. The overall trade deficit would then increase to $356 million.

d Official Cuban data from JUCEPLAN differ from IMF data, the Cuban figure being $105 million. The overall trade deficit would then increase to $307 million.

Sources: "Cuba's Foreign Trade," *Panorama Economico Latinamericano,* no. 185 (1967). pp. 4–9; United Nations, *Yearbook of International Trade Statistics 1961,* pp. 180; JUCEPLAN, *Boletín Estadístico, 1966,* pp. 124–125; JUCEPLAN, *Compendio Estadístico de Cuba, 1968,* p. 26. International Monetary Fund, *Direction of Trade, Annual 1961–1965,* pp. 308–9, and *Annual 1963–1967,* pp. 377–78; Economic Commission for Latin America, *Economic Survey of Latin America, 1963,* p. 278; International Monetary Fund, *International Financial Statistics: 1963, 1969.* January 1963 and July 1969.

Cuba's hard-currency earnings were dealt a severe blow by the loss of the American market. The nature of international sugar-marketing arrangements prevented sizable sales to other hard-currency purchasers. Negotiated contractual arrangements between sugar-producing nations and large sugar consumers account for the bulk of the international trade. The "world sugar market" is small relative to total world production, and it is a residual market in which the buying and selling of sugar not already contracted for occurs. Price fluctuations are frequent and wide. Throughout most of the 1960s (1963–64 being the major exception) prices on the world market were generally low. Because the Western European nations already had sugar suppliers, sales of Cuba's relatively large crops on the world market would have significantly depressed prices, thus netting Cuba minimal hard-currency earnings.

On the supply side, Cuban production was dealt another major blow, this one caused by internal production dislocations resulting from the embargo. These will be discussed in detail in the next section. Consequently, both supply and demand conditions placed Cuba in a precarious position with respect to hard-currency earnings, which in 1959 accounted for roughly 98 percent of export revenues, or almost $625 million. These fell drastically and by 1966 were estimated at only $110 million.[8] Without meaningful hard-currency reserves, significant import expansions from nonboycotting Western nations were virtually precluded. With rapidly declining export revenues, imports would have had to be drastically curtailed. At this point political and ideological considerations brought the socialist bloc—and large-scale grants and aid—into the picture.[9] Table 3 indicates that since 1961 Cuba has sustained large and continuous trade deficits with the bloc, financed by a variety of grants and credit schemes.[10] The import surplus represents bloc supplies without a *quid pro quo*, since it is likely Cuba's debt to the supplying countries will not be paid.

The balance of payments impact is obvious. The switch from slight trade surpluses (Table 1) to substantial deficits has given the island a serious balance-of-payments problem. Foreign debt has mushroomed, perhaps reaching as high as four billion dollars. The boycott has further contributed to the overall payments deficit by halting the significant flow of high-spending American tourists. In addition, the embargo has including blacklisting Western vessels that carry cargoes to or from Cuba. The larger companies, threatened with the possible loss of U.S. trade if shippers provide service to Cuba, have refused to deal with the island. This has resulted in higher transport costs for Western ships, essentially due to (a) the more frequent use of smaller, high-cost operators; (b) the need to pay a profit premium to induce shippers to risk loss of U.S. cargoes; and (c) higher average costs resulting from the frequent inability to utilize full carrying capacity. (Ships going to Cuba cannot generally load or unload at neighboring ports and are thus unable to utilize space fully by picking up or discharging other cargoes.) Indeed, in his July 26, 1970 speech, Castro specifically mentioned "difficulties in securing ships to move our import and export cargo. . . ."[11]

In an attempt to mitigate balance-of-payments difficulties, Castro quickly introduced exchange controls. Luxury imports were curtailed, Cuban tourist expenditures were severely reduced, an economizing and reclamation campaign was begun for all imported products, and many other similar measures were implemented. Last, it should be noted that the expropriations of U.S. citizens' property in Cuba brought Castro a balance of payments windfall, in that dividend and interest remittances abroad—formerly substantial debit items—ceased. Despite these factors, huge balance-of-payments deficits have constrained import volumes. These, in turn, have had significant repercussions upon domestic consumption and production.

The geographic location of the socialist bloc has had a large economic impact. Transport costs have increased enormously. Rather than getting supplies from its immediate neighbors, Cuba has channeled its trade to the most distant portions of the globe. Since most of this trade has been transported in foreign vessels—mostly Communist ships but also in Western ones—the invisibles account has tended toward greater deficit. This has also reduced the real value of socialist bloc aid as well as the real value of total imports, since much greater amounts are expended for transport than previously. Unfortunately, no data are available on just how much more this amount might be; two important items, however, illustrate the greater expenses involved.

Before the embargo Cuba obtained its petroleum from Venezuela, paying what would have cost an estimated $1.10 per ton transport. Although the rates of socialist transport agencies are not known, the Western rates for Odessa-to-Santiago oil shipments would have been approximately $6.50 per ton.[12] Thus, the reorientation of trade has resulted in an enormous increase in yearly transport costs. Of course, it is not Cuba alone that has absorbed all these increased costs, and it is possible that the real costs of ocean tanker transport for the Soviets may be lower than in the West. Nevertheless, a very considerable increase in freight expense must result. Another illustration is that of rice. Large amounts of rice previously were imported from the American Gulf states, but later from China. Again using Western rates, it is estimated that the cost per ton to ship rice from New Orleans to Cuba would have been about $3.50, while the corresponding rate from China to Cuba was a minimum of $12.00.[13] This would increase the transport costs for the import of rice alone in 1965 by $2.1 million, while the increases in 1964 and 1966 were slightly less than $1.2 million each year. Remembering that vast quantities of other goods formerly imported from the United States now come from such distant shores, it is obvious that the increase in transport expense has been enormous, probably tripling.[14] For 1963, then, transport costs were roughly $50 million greater than would otherwise have been the case.[15] This appears to be a reasonable annual figure (probably conservative) for the years beginning with 1963—a cost directly attributable to the boycott. These expenses continue to the present and have been mentioned in a number of Castro's public addresses, with frequent references to "hundreds of millions in additional freight charges." Manuel Céspedes, Cuban Minister of Mining, Fuels, and Metallurgy, complained in late 1974 that the "freight charges for such long-distance shipping are very high."[16] It should be stressed, however, that Cuba is financing most of these increased charges by using bloc credits rather than direct outlays. Consequently, this cost of the embargo has, in large part, been shifted to third parties, the nations of the Soviet bloc.

The 1970s have witnessed few changes in Cuba's trade patterns. "In 1974, 83% of international trade was concentrated in eleven countries, with trade being heavily biased towards the communist countries."[17] The U.S.S.R. remains the overwhelmingly dominant trade partner. Japan and Spain are the major nonbloc nations trading with Cuba, and Canada is next. For a period in the early 1970s (1973 and 1974 in particular) rising sugar prices allowed positive net trade balances. On the whole, however, hard-currency problems have continued to plague the island.

Despite the fact that Cuba's direct exchange with the Western Hemisphere (excluding Canada and Mexico) was all but terminated, it is not necessarily true that neither United States nor Latin American products have ceased to reach Cuban shores. The possibilty exists that American regulations have been contravened, either by U.S. citizens or by those in third countries. While the extent of such clandestine operations is indeterminable, some data are available that shed light on these activities.

The U.S. Department of Commerce has denied American export privileges to dozens of firms and/or individuals for transporting (or attempting to transport) American goods to Cuba. Export privileges (the privilege to buy American products) have been denied to citizens and companies of the Netherlands, Canada, Great Britain, and Mexico. American companies have also been penalized. The value of goods known to have reached Cuba is not large. Moderate quantities have also been seized, both in the United States and elsewhere, before their final shipment to Cuba. The principal kinds of goods involved have been automotive, truck, and tractor parts, diesel parts and engines, aircraft and harvester parts, machines, and sugar and oil refinery parts and equipment. It is likely that a Cuban agency, Transimport, was established for the specific purpose of clandestimely importing American replacement parts.

It is certain that a great many more American items have been imported into Cuba, the reported figures being merely the iceberg's tip. In one action, in which five persons lost their export privileges because of transshipment (the import of American goods and their reexport) to Cuba, the Commerce Department reported that discovery of the scheme prevented the export of more than a quarter of a million dollars worth of equipment urgently needed for the Cuban economy. Others have been charged by the department with supplying "substantial" or "large quantities" of American equipment, although no precise, or even estimated, values were provided. There is substantial evidence that considerably more transshipments, especially through Mexico, Canada, Europe, and perhaps Japan, have occurred, although sufficient proof for successful prosecution is often difficult to obtain. Thus, of the new equipment installed in early 1969 in one Cuban sugar mill, the major item was a diffusion system (built by a French concern) that had an American-made reduction gear motor as one of its essential parts.

The most common means of contravening the export regulations is to ship American goods to foreign companies, which then either directly reexport to Cuba (despite their affidavits to the contrary) or to sell to other firms that then export the merchandise to Cuba. Detection of these activities is difficult due to the multitude of transactions, companies, and countries involved as well as the ease of hiding such activities. Frequently, "dummy" organizations are established for the express purpose of reexport to Cuba; in other instances the Cuban operations are simply one of many. Foreign firms with American business ties have also established separate companies to export their own (non-American) products to Cuba because they feared that direct Cuban contacts might offend their American customers or bring problems with the United States government.

These clandestine operations have apparently been very profitable, for the Cuban authorities have been in desperate need of many American items. The importance of American goods and the potential profit involved is perhaps indicated by the fact that items of significant weight, such as diesel engines, have been shipped from the United States to Rotterdam and then back across the Atlantic to Cuba. In the 1970s U.S. soybeans were exported to Cuba via Holland, raising the total purchase costs by an estimated 30 percent. There is also evidence of direct trade—smuggling—from Florida locations.

The volume of transshipments cannot be accurately determined. It is reported that a group of Soviet economists who were unhappy with Cuba's continued reliance upon American products estimated that in one month alone—October 1964—Cuba imported $160,000 of smuggled United States products. Assuming this figure to be valid, it is not possible to generalize because it is not known whether this represented a normal or atypical month.

Domestic Dislocations and Impacts

Production Effects

The importance of imports, generally some 25 to 30 percent of the national product, was succinctly summarized by Boorstein in 1968:

About \$125–150 million worth of basic foodstuffs were imported, including wheat and flour, lard and other fats and oils, rice, beans, peas, onions, garlic, potatoes, and codfish. Some of these, like wheat, could not be produced in the required amounts. Tens of millions of dollars of medicines and drugs had to be imported. . . . Industry needed over \$250 million of imported parts and raw materials. . . . The buses, railroads, telephone and electric power industries, television and radio stations, and water supply systems needed spare parts. . . . And finally, thousands of miscellaneous small articles were needed—razor blades, pencils, toothbrushes, screws, electric power plugs and switches, files for sharpening the machetes of the cane-cutters.[18]

Imports, in short, were vital to maintaining the Cuban standard of living and to the island's economic growth and development. These imports had historically been supplied by the United States, creating technical and even psychological ties that could not be broken without significant disruptive effects. Shaffer and Mitchell describe Cuba's dependence as follows:

For decades the economic life-blood of the anemic island has flown through the umbilical cord that linked her with the United States. Cuban workers worked in factories equipped with American machinery; Cuban peasants toiled on plantations equipped with American agricultural implements and they produced sugar and tobacco for the American market; Cuba's middle-classes drove American cars, fitted with American tires, batteries, and sparkplugs, kept their food cool in American refrigerators . . . screwed American light bulbs into American sockets. . . .[19]

The American embargo, coupled with tactical maneuvers in the East-West confrontation, has caused the socialist bloc to replace the United States as the major supplier. Besides the resulting bilateral channeling of trade and increased transport expenses, there have been numerous domestic production problems and inconveniences to consumers resulting from the new trade relationships. Many of these problems stem from a lack of complementarity between Cuba's import needs and bloc export abilities. Often the kind of machinery and raw materials imports that Cuba needed most were the very ones in short supply within the bloc. Further, the "Cubans were shocked to discover that the Eastern countries were far behind the United States in technology, and therefore incapable of providing suitable infrastructure for the Cuban economy."[20] Not infrequently, the quality of the import was unsuitable, either because of the new suppliers' poor production processes or simply because the goods—perfectly usable within the bloc—were not adapted to the Cuban climate, technological orientations, or methods of use. The kind of wheat sent to Cuba did not work well in the Cuban mills. Hundreds of pieces of Soviet farm equipment have had to be junked because they were designed for continental crops planted in rows of different widths from those of Cuban practices. K.S. Karol has written of Ernesto "Che" Guevara's shock upon learning that a factory imported from Poland required 270 workers to produce an amount equivalent to what 25 workers could produce in a Western factory.[21] The list of examples is almost limitless and is known only too well by the Cuban producer and consumer.

Then, too, the changeover to the metric system and the language and cultural barriers created problems that had to be transcended by those Cubans in charge of import orders. Mistakes in ordering and incomplete fulfillment of orders have been frequent. Further, delays and time lapses between orders and deliveries have repeatedly disrupted production schedules. Finally, there have been serious spare parts shortages, both for bloc-supplied goods and for U.S.-produced items; parts for the latter can usually be obtained only through smuggling.

Although many developing nations have parts problems, Cuba's merit special attention. The country was dependent upon U.S. suppliers because Cuba's capital stock came almost wholly from the United States, as did the bulk of its raw materials and technological methods. Since "different equipment and parts belonged to different technological systems,"[22] the Soviet bloc suppliers who supplanted American sources were unable to service adequately Cuba's existing capital stock. This has resulted in two distinct and costly kinds of economic impacts. The first comprises indirect costs. The lack of spare parts disrupted production and idled land, labor, and capital. These interruptions adversely affected other industries, with the extent of disruption depending upon the degree of linkage with the rest of the economy. In short, the economy moved away from its production-possibilities frontier (graphically, from a point on or near the frontier to one farther inward, closer to the origin). Second, there were capital effects. The production frontier itself moved inward because much equipment was rendered unusable by a lack of parts or specifically designed material inputs. In economic terms the embargo of parts has had the same effect as pinpoint bombings or industrial sabotage—capital equipment has been rendered economically useless (although left intact physically).[23]

It is difficult to realize or fully comprehend the acute problems caused by the lack of spare parts, replacement equipment, and normal raw materials. Even a brief survey of the Cuban press during the 1960s shows it to be filled with notices of new repair shops, editorials on the need to economize on items in short supply, and articles concerning conservation of raw materials. Indeed, these themes were as recurrent as the weather and international politics. While many of the articles—of which a typical title was, "Mincin Employees Solving Problems of Automobile Spare Parts"[24]—were in part exhortations for further economizing of scarce items, they reflected real needs and indicated the multitude of steps taken to combat boycott-related difficulties.

It is no overstatement to repeat that Cuba's entire industrial structure—including the transport, communications, power, mining, and agricultural sectors—was vitally dependent upon American parts and raw materials. Indeed, "most of the larger factories worked with raw materials . . . sometimes specifically designed for the machinery and processes in which they were to be used."[25] Such dependence is easily visualized:

> Just as an automobile can be put out of commission for lack of some small, inexpensive part—say a gasket for a brake cylinder worth three dollars—so the operations of a large factory or mine, turning out products worth several million dollars a year, can be halted by the absence of ordinarily insignificant pieces of equipment. The unavailability of a small filter—worth $25—for equipment at Moa which pulverized the ore into a fine powder can stop the operations of the whole

nickel plant. The failure of small parts for the ventilators, or the overhead cable system which moves the copper around, can interfere with production at the Matahambre copper mine. There are thousands of such parts throughout the mines, factories, and electric power and telephone systems of Cuba.[26]

It is not possible to quantify accurately the opportunity costs of lost production due to work stoppages caused by breakdowns and a lack of spare parts. The Cuban authorities themselves do not have complete statistics, although for particular segments of the economy, for particular periods, some data are available. Just a few instances will illustrate the seriousness of this problem and the potential output lost. The transportation industry was particularly crippled. "One-quarter of the island's busses were out of operation for want of spare parts late in 1961. Only one-half of Cuba's 1,400 railroad passenger cars were functioning in 1962. . . ."[27] For lack of spare parts only 25 percent of the rolling stock in use in 1959 was still in service by 1971.[28] Previously, there had been approximately 2,000 busses serving the greater Havana area. Over one period breakdowns had been "running at an average of 280 daily, that is, over 7,000 per month. Over 400 buses were out of action with serious defects."[29] Indeed, so severe was the damage in this sector that 2,665 buses had to be imported during the 1963–67 period.[30]

Parts problems became so acute in the 1960s that Cubans started dismantling existing mechanical devices to utilize their working parts to salvage other machines. An active black market in automobile parts and accessories has been operating for years. Cars have been destroyed through cannibalization because the parts have become so valuable. Thousands of junked cars littered the Havana area for years. In 1967 the bill for spare parts for cars and jeeps totalled 3.2 million pesos.[31]

The sugar industry was particulaly affected, especially by the failure of the transport system and mill breakdowns. A 1964 British study concerning the mechanization of agriculture reported the following:

> Caterpillar tractors not in operation due to lack of spare parts constitute 62 percent of the total, of which 37 percent were manufactured in capitalistic countries and 25 percent in socialist countries. Wheel tractors paralyzed because they are

not in working condition amount to 47 percent of the total, of
which 31 percent came from capitalistic countries and 16
percent from socialist countries. There are more than 200
tractors inoperative in the Oriente Province because of lack of
tires. . . . In Camaguey, 220 Caterpillars have been laid aside
due to the lack of spare parts and 622 due to lack of tires.[32]

A 1967 case study of the Ecuador Sugar Mill indicates that as late
as that year it still had eleven American-made boilers. The report
stated: "The spare parts situation is serious and stoppages and
malfunctions are frequent."[33] In another mill, the Hermanos Díaz
refinery, all but one of thirty-nine storage tanks were of American
manufacture. Four were considered in extremely poor condition,
thirteen in poor condition, five in fair condition, and eleven in good
condition. The one Soviet-made tank was reported to be leaking.
Most of the tanks still in good condition were the smaller ones, so
that the overall capacity was poor and the refinery operated
ineffectively although it was still functioning.[34] Spare parts for
American-made equipment have been brought in by way of
Canada, Mexico, and Great Britain. By 1965 nine sugar mills had
been cannibalized. Of the 161 mills existing in 1969, Mesa-Lago
reports that only 115 still functioned in April 1972.[35] Undoubtedly,
this lost capacity, among other factors, contributed to the failure to
attain the ten-million-ton goal set by Castro for 1970.

Work stoppages and breakdowns have been caused by other
boycott-related problems, in addition to those already mentioned.
As indicated, a great deal of improvisation has taken place. New
fuels have been introduced and the reuse of lubricants and fuels
developed; these substitutes, however, are generally of very poor
quality and therefore tend to increase the rate of decay of many
machines. In addition, where raw materials could be obtained from
the socialist countries, timing problems played havoc with
production schedules. The trip from China normally takes two
months and deliveries are notoriously late, as frequently is also the
case with Soviet shipments. Often catalogs have been unavailable
for the products of the socialist countries, and ordering parts is
virtually impossible.

The absence of United States technical expertise has been quite
damaging. It "was precisely in the most technically advanced
sectors . . . where communication with the U.S. was easy and
rapid, that Cuban technicians had been both unnecessary and

unavailable."[36] Even today, when breakdowns occur or advisers are needed, too few are available: the Cubans need more training in the area, the Americans are boycotting, and the Russians are not making efforts to become more familiar with the problems.

Other costs are involved as well. The nation has become repair oriented, and a disproportionate amount of resources is devoted to this kind of activity. Repair shops are everywhere and are continuously busy. Such employment, however, would have been unnecessary in the absence of boycott and represents substantial opportunity cost in terms of other outputs foregone. In addition, the great distance between Cuba and her new suppliers means that only bulk shipments are feasible rather than the traditional Cuban order from the United States, which could be sent in almost any size delivery. Because Cuba did not possess adequate port and warehousing facilities to receive large shipments, investment funds have had to be channeled into this area rather than into more directly productive sectors. Even as late as April 1971, Castro reported that much imported equipment lay unused or had rusted on the docks, partly because of inadequate warehousing facilities. In short, Cuba's industry and agriculture have been in a state of intermittent paralysis. Far more than just the sugar industry is involved: the production of rayon, tires and tubes, nickel, and other items has come to frequent stops, often lasting for months.[37]

Despite these many examples, the lack of reliable data for the entire economy makes any estimate of the total output foregone highly suspect.[38] What can be said of "capital effects."? The production possibilities frontier clearly shrank because of involuntary accelerated capital consumption. Here we can be more specific and attempt meaningful estimates. This writer's investigations suggest that rates of capital consumption in Cuba at least doubled or tripled during the first six years of the embargo, particularly during the middle and latter years when stocks of parts and raw materials became depleted. Such accelerated rates may have continued through the later 1960s. Assuming an incremental capital/output ratio of 3:1, then, and using 6 percent[39] as the normal average annual depreciation, a doubling of capital consumption rates would reduce growth rates in national product by 2 points. Thus, if total investment were 18 percent of the national product, normal growth would be 4 percent; under boycott-induced accelerated depreciation, growth falls to 2 percent. If the rate of gross investment were 15 percent, growth would fall from 3 percent to 1 percent. If capital consumption tripled, growth would be retarded by 4 points, that is, if normal growth had been 4 percent, it would have been reduced to zero. If we are more conservative and use a normal annual capital consumption rate of 4 percent, a doubling of this rate cuts growth by 1.33 (from 4 percent to 2.67 percent or from 3.67 percent to 2.33 percent). If the capital/output ratio were higher, say 4:1, an 18 percent rate of investment with 6 percent normal depreciation would yield 3 percent growth; a doubling of depreciation would reduce growth to 1.5 percent, and a tripling would reduce growth to zero.[40] From this line of reasoning, three conclusions are obvious; (1) the greater the embargo-induced accelerated capital consumption, the greater the output lost; (2) the lower the normal annual rates of capital consumption, the less the output lost; and (3) the higher the capital/output ratio, the less the output lost. It is this writer's belief that a reduction in the Cuban rate of growth of some 2–3 points is the most probable figure. It must be stressed that *such declines are due to shrinkage of the production possibilities frontier alone* and are separate from other aspects of the embargo.

Although exact growth rates for Cuba since 1960 are not available, a wide variety of estimates all point to serious growth deficiencies. Mesa-Lago's research indicates that after a general stagnation in 1961, the economy dipped precipitously in 1962 and 1963 (years of serious spare parts shortages), recovered in 1964 (without reaching the 1960–61 levels), stagnated again in 1965, and declined once again in 1966.[41] Another source suggests that per capita GNP in 1966 was 4 percent lower than in 1962.[42] Of course, these aggregate statistical findings must be tempered by several considerations unrelated to the embargo that may also have retarded growth, such as radical institutional reorganizations, both political and economic; possible inadequacies and/or errors in economic planning; the loss of population through emigration; and adverse weather conditions, just to name a few.[43]

One further point with regard to investment capacity merits note. As Wolfgang Stolper has pointed out, "The level of investments depends also upon the availability of imported complementary goods."[44] This is a purely technical relationship. Furtado notes that "this dependency occurs . . . mainly in regard to the transformation of savings into real investments."[45] Table 2 indicated the important role of producer goods imports for Cuba. Since the embargo has reduced Cuba's ability to import from traditional suppliers, while at the same time bloc imports have been found inappropriate or inferior, the level of current investment has been held to levels lower than otherwise possible in the absence of an embargo. To summarize, the embargo has acted to depress total investment, and, as mentioned above, that portion of gross investment allocated to replacement has been magnified significantly.

Consumption Effects

In addition to the growth-retarding factors related to the boycott, the general quality of output has deteriorated very seriously because of three main factors: (1) the excessively rapid rates of import substitution forced by the embargo; (2) the necessary domestic economizing that has occurred; (3) the lack of complementarity with new supplies.[46] When examining the first factor, it should be remembered that from the outset Castro was determined to lessen dependence upon both the United States and sugar. Therefore, domestic diversification and the accompanying import substitution would have resulted even if no embargo had been instituted. In a few areas such efforts would have been economically rational; however, the boycott's denial to Cuba both of American finished and semifinished goods, coupled with smaller foreign exchange earnings for purchases from other suppliers, meant that rapid import substitution—on a large rather than restricted scale—was necessary. Referring to the limits to successful import substitution, one study has concluded:

> These limits, however, can be quickly exceeded. . . . Import substitution may therefore soon spread a country's resources too thin over numerous small and inefficient enterprises, and extend to types of production ill suited to its conditions, with the unfortunate result of raising costs even in industries in which it should otherwise be able to compete.[47]

This is a remarkably close description of the pattern of import substitution in Cuba during the 1960s. Such efforts have been extremely costly and have resulted in a sharp deterioration in the quality of many goods. Cuba's problems in this regard are not unique; other developing nations have experienced similar difficulties[48]; however, Cuba's circumstances were further frustrated by the embargo.

Quality also suffered due to domestic economizing efforts, which became necessary in 1961 when severe goods shortages began to appear. Most tires, for example, are recapped and a whole host of items normally discarded are reused or reconstructed. Recovery efforts are widespread in oil utilization. A Cuban source reports:

> We save great quantities of foreign credits through this process because our lubricants come from abroad and all the re-refined oil we can obtain, about 72 percent of the total, can be used again as lubricant.[49]

This use of lower-quality items, though, not only increases maintenance problems but also tends to accelerate deterioration of existing capital stock.

Finally, a lack of complementarity with Cuba's new trading partners has also contributed to accelerated capital consumption and lower-quality outputs. As is well known, the Soviet Union has itself had serious problems in maintaining quality standards, and export items are no exception. Quality, therefore, has declined due to the substitution of suppliers—from relatively high-quality sources to ones of much poorer quality. In addition, even Soviet products—particularly agricultural machinery and motors—that are constructed according to proper minimum standards have encountered difficulties in the Cuban climate and terrain. Perhaps most important, the new trading partners have been unable to supply certain raw material inputs at all, have provided less suitable substitutes (though not necessarily of low quality), or have been unable to supply sufficient quantities.

Examples of quality deterioration are plentiful. For example, not only is there a shortage of soaps but those available are not scented because the fragrance-imparting ingredients are not domestically produced. Cuban raw materials must be utilized in glass bottle production, and the color is often caramel rather than clear. Glue does not dry well and often several matches must be struck before one lights. Che Guevara's comments with respect to soft drinks are classic:

> Coca-Cola was one of the most popular drinks in Cuba, but today it tastes like cough syrup. It has seven, eight, or

nine . . . ingredients. . . . It was found neccessary to do much investigation and a substitute has been found, but sometimes we have to eliminate an ingredient that we can't make. It is necessary to work harder because we have to make sure of a quality product in quantities sufficient for the whole people to consume. . . . Soft drinks in Cuba are almost a necessity, given the climate.[50]

One final example—toothpaste—shows how quality deterioration affects the average Cuban. Quoting again from Che Guevara,

There is at present a scarcity of toothpaste. . . . Since about four months ago there has been a paralysis in production; there was, however, a large stock. . . . Afterwards the reserves began to decline and the raw material did not arrive. . . . When the raw material—bicalcium sulfate—did arrive, it did not meet the specifications for making toothpaste. The technical comrades of the enterprises got to work and made a toothpaste . . . it is a toothpaste as good as the old one, it cleans equally well, but after a month it becomes hard.[51]

Such problems are a direct result of the boycott and Cuba's previously close trade ties with the United States.

In addition, the traditional pattern of comsumption has been markedly altered. "Successive waves of United States exports and investments pushed the Cubans into United States consumption patterns, which they could not easily change."[52] Indeed, it is likely that "few foreign consumers . . . were as committed to our kinds of products."[53] It should be noted that when the 1903 Reciprocity Treaty between Cuba and the United States was implemented, allowing mutual tariff reductions, the absolute volume of Cuban imports from traditional suppliers in Europe did not diminish, mainly due to the consumption habits and patterns of the Cuban people, which could not change as quickly as legislative enactments. Only over time did a new orientation occur, with American products gradually supplanting the older ones. The abrupt cessation of American imports in the 1960s, then, seriously disrupted traditional patterns of consumption, although the relatively large stocks of commodities on hand did provide a cushion for several months. Nevertheless, shortages soon appeared for products such as toothpaste, soft drinks, razor blades, soaps, colognes, chicken, meats, lard, vegetables, and a host of other items. For example, imports of chickens from the United States normally ranged between 1.2 million to 1.5 million monthly, supplying almost the entire Cuban market.[54] After the embargo this quantity fell to zero, and Cuban farms had nowhere near the capacity to supply the normal demand, let alone one inflated by income redistribution measures. The absence of chicken increased demand for meat, which also disappeared from the market. Funds were then channeled into fish, and again severe shortages appeared. Such shortages soon extended to almost all goods.[55] In March 1961, general food rationing was introduced.[56]

Again, Soviet and socialist bloc supplies, although providing a means of subsistence, in many instances resulted in sharp changes in Cuban consumption patterns. Cuba was traditionally a very heavy lard consumer. With U.S. supplies terminated, a change in the Cuban diet was necessitated. Domestic production of lard and vegetable oils increased to cope with shortages, while Castro himself campaigned against heavy consumption of lard, charging that the average Cuban's lard consumption was excessive and detrimental to good health. Another example is rice, also important in the Cuban diet. When the American supplies were cut, China began to supply rice, although in insufficient quantities. After political tensions between Cuba and China arose, despite Cuba's significantly greater needs for rice due to domestic dislocations, China reduced her supplies drastically. Castro then spoke to the Cuban people of China's "treachery" and collusion with the "imperialists," and this time suggested that rice be voluntarily dropped from the diet because more nutritional foods—from the U.S.S.R.—were becoming available! Despite trade fairs and promotion of Soviet goods, Cubans have only reluctantly changed patterns of consumption, essentially because alternative products have simply been unavailable in sufficient quantities. A 1969 report is indicative of the scope of rationing and general conditions in Cuba:

> In addition to the long list of items already rationed, Cubans will now be limited to 6 lb. of sugar a month. Smokers will have to content themselves with one pack of Virginia cigarettes or two packets of tobacco per week. Over Christmas housewives formed queues for their ration of three toys for each child under 13 years old and the nightclubs were

temporarily opened. The government tries to buoy up spirits by promising a definite improvement in living conditions in 1970 to coincide with the hoped-for 10 million-ton sugar crop and the maturity of the 500,000 head dairy herd, which it is hoped will end milk rationing.[57]

The 10-million-ton crop, of course, failed to materialize and the availability of consumer goods today remains substantially unchanged. In 1977, for example, the meat ration was twelve ounces every ten days (if available), coffee, one ounce per week and rice, 6 pounds per month.

Foregone potential costs without doubt are relevant, but basically conjectural. Cuba's tourist industry, for example, in the absence of the embargo (and positive efforts by Castro to discourage Americans) would probably have enjoyed continued growth. Today Cuba is attempting to rebuild its tourist industry and since late 1977 has tried to attract Americans. A few other industries may also fall into this category.

Summary and Conclusions

Changes in national production are a function of a variety of factors, probably the foremost being changes in the size and qualitative aspects of the labor force, changes in the size of the capital stock, changed rates of input utilization, differing terms of trade in external commerce, and changes in technology. These factors, together with others, shape the course of national output. The embargo has strongly influenced at least three of these factors. The embargo-induced deterioration of Cuba's capital stock probably decreased annual growth rates by 2 points or more. The terms of trade certainly worsened, particularly in terms of the economic cost of procuring supplies from more distant sources. Extra transport costs alone were estimated at $50 million for 1963. The exact gross barter terms of trade are not known due to the nature of the bilateral agreements and methods of financing. The quality of the new imports and their usefulness as substitutes for the goods (particularly inputs) they replaced have been far from satisfactory. To the degree that socialist bloc credit arrangements have financed the increased transport costs and Cuban deficits, this represents a subsidy. The costs of the embargo continue but are absorbed or have been shifted, at least in part, to Cuba's socialist trade partners. Growth of output was also seriously retarded by boycott-induced unemployment of all factors of production; however, quantitative estimates of these losses are impossible to make.

The hurried program of widespread import substitution has proved quite costly. Further, significant productive efforts have had to be diverted to repair work, reuse of materials, fuels, and lubricants, and to warehouse and storage facilities. Last, consumption patterns have been forced to change and the general quality of output has seriously deteriorated. These general costs are obviously subjective, but nonetheless real.

The World Bank in 1973 estimated Cuba's GNP growth over the 1960–71 period at an average annual rate of −1.2 percent.[58] As mentioned earlier, such estimates reflect the influence of *all* growth variables. The massive emigration, adverse weather conditions, errors in planning, and numerous other retarding factors, including the embargo, contributed to this negative performance. Almost all previous research, however, has ignored the pervasive impacts of the boycott and has tended to concentrate on errors in planning, ideological biases, bureaucratic interferences, and so forth.[59]

Socialist bloc support has resulted in a huge amount of foreign indebtedness[60] and a dependence upon present communist suppliers which is even greater than the previous reliance upon the United States. Despite this extreme economic dependence upon the bloc, Cuba appears to have been able to maintain relative autonomy in its decision making.[61]

In essence, the embargo is a multinational agreement to refrain from economic intercourse. As is well known, all such arrangements are subject to possible secret cheating, in a variety of forms, that may eventually lead to overt noncompliance and the total breakdown of the collective nature of the sanctions. Acquiescence by Western European governments to U.S. pressures and requests ended in 1964, with the British sale of Leyland's buses marking one of the first major open acts of noncompliance. In that same year twenty-one of the twenty-two members of the O.A.S. implemented economic sanctions. However, over the years, more and more Latin American states have reestablished political and economic relations with Cuba, despite O.A.S. sanctions. Finally the O.A.S. voted to end its economic and diplomatic sanctions in July 1975 (sixteen countries, including the United States, approved), although individual member states were free to continue their own boycotts. The United States continued its embargo but announced in August 1975 that overseas subsidiaries of American companies would be permitted to trade with Cuba. The previous prohibition had proved difficult to enforce and had engendered antagonism from the governments of the countries in which the subsidiaries were operating. Since that date there have been further relaxations in the American embargo. American politicians and industrial leaders visited Cuba in 1976 and 1977, and the first tourist excursions to be permitted from the United States began in December 1977 and January 1978. Cuba is hoping to rebuild its tourist industry and enhance its hard-currency earnings.

Interestingly, the American sanctions relaxations have continued despite erratic political relations with the Castro regime. For example, in the face of the August 1975 trade ban modifications, Cuba issued in September a number of pronouncements in support of Puerto Rican independence. Further, much to U.S. chagrin, Cuban involvement in Angola and elsewhere in Africa has heightened. Although Castro has intermittently made gestures of accommodation, his foreign policies are apparently impervious to embargo modifications. Yet both Castro and numerous U.S. officials (under both the Ford and Carter administrations) have indicated a desire to end the boycott and reestablish commercial ties. It would appear that American economic pressures have had little impact upon Castro's domestic orientation and his foreign policies, despite its great economic effectiveness. Cyrus Vance, U.S. Secretary of State, has termed the embargo a "failure."[62] Sanctions, then, have been economically effective, yet politically unsuccessful.

What factors may account for the progressive reestablishment of trade ties by Latin American states and the ultimate lifting of the embargo by the O.A.S.? Because trade is a two-way street, it is not generally possible for nations to impose boycotts upon others without in some way impairing their own economic welfare. Hence, economic considerations in the boycotting states have a role to play. Peru, Argentina, Jamaica, Guyana, Barbados, and others reestablished commercial ties in the 1970s prior to the

O.A.S. decision. The significant rise in the world price of sugar during that period no doubt was a factor, for it allowed Cuba, despite its sugar obligations to the Soviets, to have some $1.5 billion (1974) of sugar revenue at its disposal. For many Latin American states Cuban trade became too important to ignore. In 1976, for example, the sale of 100,000 tons of sugar to Venezuela was arranged, the first transaction since relations between the two countries were restored in 1975. There were also political considerations. Argentina, both for domestic purposes and as a means of asserting Latin American leadership (by defying Washington) granted Cuba trade credits. Other governments, perhaps believing the embargo was soon to be lifted, preferred to be forerunners rather than simply following the U.S. or O.A.S. lead. Last, attitudes toward the embargo changed because it had been unsuccessful in either removing Castro or getting him to change his policies.[63]

The United States has been the most important boycotting nation by far and can continue the embargo unilaterally, but these sanctions do and will continue to have steadily diminished impacts, particularly because the proportion of American-made infrastructure and capital goods is constantly falling. If the economic "stick" has been unsuccessful (with regard to the political goals) thus far, its possibilities for future success are even more remote.

Recognizing the very severe damage that sanctions have inflicted is likely to temper some commonplace views and generalizations concerning Cuba. For example, it has been popular in the United States to claim that "communism in Cuba has failed," or that prosperity and socialism do not mix. This, of course, exemplifies the *post hoc* fallacy. *Under any system—capitalism, socialism, communism—a Cuba under such sanctions would have had extreme difficulty demonstrating meaningful, if any, progress.* Whether its present institutional arrangements have mitigated or exacerbated Cuba's economic woes is another question altogether, and one which is likely to be debated hotly for some time.

Cuba's ability to survive despite sanctions also clearly indicates the limits to using American economic power for coercive purposes. Few states could have been more vulnerable, given the great dependence upon the United States. All the cost categories—direct, indirect, foregone potential, and capital effects—experienced significant negative impacts. Yet neither the

Castro government nor the new socioeconomic system seem likely to topple.

In summary, the embargo has been quite economically damaging, although much of its incidence has been shifted to the socialist bloc. Its political results, on the other hand, have been questionable. Indeed, the absolute refusal to trade with Cuba literally forced and cemented almost permanent relations with the Communist world. In the absence of the boycott, it is quite likely that Castro's economic relations with these states would not have assumed significant proportions. If the fledgling economic ties had been a mere "flirtation" rather than a marriage, it is interesting to speculate what impact continued trade relations with the U.S. would have had upon Castro's personal views and policies. One final point: the findings of this chapter should not be interpreted to mean that all of Cuba's economic problems stem, either directly or indirectly, from the embargo. Internal factors, more or less autonomously generated, have also played a major role. The basic point is that the embargo's effects have been very substantial, with negative impacts permeating virtually all aspects of Cuban life. It is to be hoped that future studies will be able to quantify the influence of the other considerations, so that the relative influence of all variables can be pictured and assessed in their proper perspectives.

4

The Arab Boycott of Israel

The Arab boycott of Israel is another, and much older, attempt at regional economic sanctions. At first glance, one might guess that such an embargo would be quite effective since Israel is surrounded on three sides by boycotting Arab nations. Hence, all overland and pipeline methods of transport are blocked. This certainly has caused problems and is the chief source of direct costs. Indirect costs, on the other hand, have been minimal, since subtitute suppliers and markets have been found. The surrounding Arab states supplied almost none of Israel's infrastructure, so capital effects—a major ingredient in the Cuban embargo—are totally absent. Foregone potential costs are quite significant and will be discussed below.

The Arab states, with the exception of Egypt, have not recognized Israel's right to exist: "The interpretation given by the League [Arab League, see Figure 2] is that the boycott will bring about the eventual economic collapse of the state of Israel and will reveal that it is not economically viable in the midst of a hostile world."[1] Quite obviously, as was also true in the Cuban situation, the boycott has not been politically successful. Israel survives and has not been coerced into any major policy changes by the embargo.

Background

When the Arab League came into being in 1944, one of its stated objectives was "to frustrate further Jewish economic development in Palestine by means of a boycott against Zionist produce."[2]

It was not, however, until early in 1946 that the boycott against

47

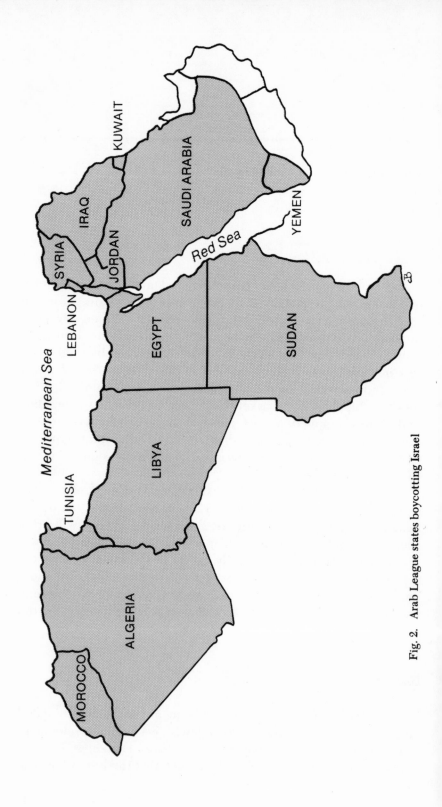

Fig. 2. Arab League states boycotting Israel

Zionist produce began. The League established a Permanent Boycott Committee and declared: "Products of Palestinian Jews are to be considered undesirable in Arab countries. They should be prohibited and refused as long as their production in Palestine might lead to the realization of Zionist political aims" (Resolution No. 16).[3] In June, Resolution No. 72 was adopted by which the League urged each member state to pass legislation to make selling of Arab lands to Zionists a crime. More steps were taken to strengthen the boycott, one of which included the establishment of boycott offices in each Arab state. Zionist services, such as banking, insurance, and transport were also to be boycotted. Resolution No. 68 urged that: "Propaganda should be carried on to make the boycott of Zionist goods a creed of the Arab nations so that each Arab might preach it enthusiastically to all."[4]

Britain ended its Mandate and open fighting between Jews and Arabs broke out in 1948, and the League sent an Arab Liberation army into the battle. Organized military action stopped in 1949, but only an armistice—not a treaty of peace—was signed. With the cessation of armed hostilties the boycott activities took on a new importance. They were to accomplish what the military campaign had failed to achieve. A general boycott office had already been established in Damascus, and the boycott mechanism was extended and more fully developed. Economic warfare replaced military hostilties, bringing the conflict to a new and broader plane.

An understanding of the impact and opportunity costs of the Arab boycott requires not only an examination of Israel's contemporary economic structure, but also some familiarity with the economic organization and trade patterns of Palestine during the first half of the twentieth century, particularly in the period of British rule.

Palestine experienced a rather remarkable growth during the approximately thirty years of the Mandate period. The population more than doubled, and the areas of cultivatable land increased by one-third. Localized urbanization occured, the Haifa port and refinery were constructed, and the general standard of living, levels of education, and health improved substantially, particularly in the urban areas. This progress has been attributed to four factors: (1) the establishment of a relatively efficient and progressive public administration by the British; (2) growth of the

Arab population and its development of social, political, and economic consciousness; (3) the settlement of Jewish immigrants and the accompanying inflows of capital and skills; and (4) World War II, which gave a great spurt to industrialization through contracts from the military and enforced trade protection.[5]

It should at this point be stressed that the term *economy of Palestine* is misleading, and any references to the entire economy may conceal as much as they reveal. The reasons for this are the economic, political, and cultural differences that characterized the Jewish and Arab sectors so that each constituted a separate and distinct community, with interrelations held to a minimum.

One fundamental contrast between the two sectors was the occupational structure and basis of earnings of each. During the 1930s, agriculture provided less than one-tenth of the income of the Jewish sector, but almost three-quarters of the non-Jewish income total.[6] Jewish per capita incomes in Palestine were significantly greater than those of the Arabs due to three factors: (1) the greater relative productivity of Jewish workers; (2) their relative concentration in the higher-income-yielding occupations; and (3) the larger proportion of workers in the Jewish sector, no doubt in large measure due to the relatively high nonparticipating rates of Arab women and to the differing age compositions of each group (higher proportion of young dependents in the Arab sector). Approximately one-fifth of those employed in the Jewish sector were engaged in agriculture during the decade of the 1930s,[7] despite the fact that agricultural pursuits yielded low per capita incomes. This high proportion resulted from the noneconomic criteria upon which Jewish agriculture was based. Zionist efforts, in short, were pursued more for social and political considerations. Jews had for centuries been deprived of the right to own land. Ingrained in Zionist ideology seemed to be a desire to allow the Jew to till the soil and develop his agricultural abilities. In addition, the desire for relative autarky was strong, particularly in view of the mutual suspicions and hostilities of the two sectors. Thus, reliance upon local Arab supplies of food was minimized, despite the rationality of comparative advantage that suggested a shift of Jewish resources out of agriculture into higher-yielding pursuits.

The occupational distribution of Jewish employment exhibited a heavy concentration in the service industries, a pattern that continued into the time of statehood. During the 1930s, 45 percent or more of employed Jews were in the service sector, principally engaged in commerce, personal services, government, and public services.[8] The major reason for this was the narrow occupational distribution of Jewish immigrants, who comprised only a small proportion of the labor force in the lands they left. Another reason, pointed out by Ofer, is that in the intersectoral trade that did occur, the Arab sector made extensive use of Jewish services, particularly those relating to trade, commerce, medicine, and other professions. Ofer explains:

> Part of the overconcentration in trade and "other public services" in the mandatory period can therefore be ascribed to the export of these services to the Arab sector. The Jewish sector was able to carry out this export because of the higher level of development and the occupational structure of its population, which gave it a comparative advantage in the supply of commercial and professional services.[9]

Unfortunately, the hostility between the two groups minimized economic intercourse. If relations between the two sectors had been normal, and if simple criteria of economic profitability had been applied, there is no doubt that there would have been much more intersectoral trade.[10]

By the end of World War I, Palestine's manufacturing development had not yet passed far beyond the handicraft stage, a fact quite understandable in light of the traditional agricultural orientation of the Arab population. However, the influx of Jews from Europe—about 452,000 between 1919 and 1948[11]—had significant impact upon Palestine's nascent manufacturing activities. As Jewish immigration increased, bringing with it capital inflows, technological skills, and entrepreneurial abilities, the manufacturing sector began to develop. By 1946, probably five-sixths of all those employed in manufacturing worked in Jewish enterprises. The use of Arab labor, however, was not great due to mutual antagonisms and the reluctance of Jewish enterprises to become dependent upon Arab help. This was particularly the case during the serious disturbances of the 1936–39 period. Because much of the labor needed was unskilled, while the productivity gap of the Arab workers was not necessarily far behind that of the more expensive Jewish laborer, the result was unnecessary cost increases. Without doubt, this retarded the development of Palestine's industry.

Most production was devoted to consumer goods sold locally. Industry was located mainly in the cities of Tel Aviv, Jerusalem, and Haifa, the areas of concentrated Jewish urban settlement. Although Arab industrial development was minor, by the late 1930s it had grown considerably. The number of persons employed was estimated at over six thousand in 1939, working in very small shops, generally without power-driven machinery.[12] In general, Arab manufactured goods were noncompetitive with those of Jewish industries "since most of the Jewish output was confined to articles not produced or used by Arabs."[13] There were some areas of common ground, such as articles of clothing, soap, cigarettes, shoes, and a few other items, but here too competition was limited because the type and quality of the goods demanded by each sector differed. Nevertheless, economic interchange did take place, the estimate being that approximately 10 percent of Jewish industrial output (composed mainly of electricity) found its way into Arab hands.[14] This estimate, however, is low as it took into account neither retail purchases of Jewish goods by local Arabs nor Jewish industrial exports to the surrounding Arab countries. Arab products penetrated the Jewish sector somewhat more easily since prices were generally lower due to lower wage costs. Finally:

> There was one important branch, namely the building trade, in which the Arabs had the advantage since they possessed a virtual monopoly in stone quarrying and dressing and in the lime industries. The investment in building was predominantly Jewish, while the supply of materials has largely been in Arab hands.[15]

Again, despite the hostility between Zionists and Arabs and mutual attempts at isolation,[16] the cost advantages of specialization and trade resulted in economic intercourse.

No discussion of Palestinian economic conditions can be complete without an investigtion of the international sector. Indeed, it has been suggested that during the decade of the 1930s the "most striking economic development . . . was the growth of foreign trade."[17] Palestine's external trade was characterized by sizable unfavorable balances, a large proportion of capital goods imports, and a heavy export concentration on one product—citrus—directed toward one market, the United Kingdom.[18] In addition, the country had a very high rate of trade per capita, one several times as great as the corresponding figures for similarly situated nations such as Egypt, Iraq, Syria or Turkey, and almost as large as those for the United Kingdom and Sweden, which were among the world's most advanced trading states.[19]

Trade, then, was extremely important. Annual imports in the 1930s averaged more than three times the value of exports; this unfavorable balance was essentially a sign of development and incipient industrialization. Also of importance was the fact that the method of financing trade imbalances—immigrant capital rather than borrowing—did not create a heavy drain on future balance-of-payments positions. Other reasons for the deficits included the demand, especially by the Jewish sector, for manufactured goods not locally produced and the insufficiency of Palestine's agricultural production relative to the nation's food requirements. Finally, the Open Door commercial policy of the Mandate government left Palestine a dumping ground for foreign producers. Domestic industry was not only given no stimulative protection, but in addition it was not allowed to protect itself from subsidized imports and other forms of discrimination.[20] The Mandate's tariff policies were opposed by both the Jewish and Arab sectors with respect to agriculture, and particularly by Jewish interests with respect to industry.

During the interwar period Palestine's import structure was dominated by manufactured articles and food. The major food items imported were wheat, wheat flour, cattle, fruits, sugar, butter, rice, sheep, goats, and fish. In terms of suppliers, the United Kingdom ranked first with 16.4 percent of Palestine's imports over the 1936–39 period. Germany and Austria supplied just over 15 percent, this source of supply being a function of Germany's insistence that Jewish capital be exported only in commodity form. Syria, the United States, and Rumania followed, with roughly 9 percent each, while Egypt supplied just under 4 percent. Manufactured goods principally came from Britain, Germany, Austria, and the United States, while the main suppliers of food and related items were Syria, Britain, Egypt, Rumania, and the United States. The United Kingdom, by virtue of its citrus purchases, absorbed more than 50 percent of total exports. Syria followed, a distant second with about 9 percent, but was Palestine's leading customer for yarns, tissues, and apparel. Holland ranked third.

In 1937 favorable trade balances existed with only three countries—Britain, Holland, and Sweden. The largest deficit was with Germany, followed by Rumania, the United States, Syria, and Egypt.[21] It should be noted that the Middle East provided 20 percent of Palestine's imports over the 1936–39 period and purchased 12 percent of its exports. The area, then, was neither a major supplier nor a major purchaser, although the trade volumes were not insignificant. This was characteristic of all the Middle Eastern states, however, and relative to them, Palestine's intra-Middle Eastern trade was large.

As has already been suggested, the relative separation of Arab and Jewish sectors minimized their economic intercourse. Nevertheless, trade did occur, with the normal flow characterized by Arab supplies of agricultural products and Jewish "exports" of manufactured goods and services. Despite the autarkic position taken by Jewish agricultural settlements, the needs of the urban communities required that between 6 and 7 percent of the Jewish food supply come from local Arab agriculture.[22] In addition, such supplies were supplemented and occasionally supplanted by agricultural produce from neighboring Arab lands. In turn, the Jewish sector provided manufactured goods, an area in which it had a comparative advantage. Manufacturing was slow to develop, and the limited output produced served essentially, although not wholly, the needs of the Jewish sector. Interestingly, "political considerations did not seriously impede the marketing of the products of Jewish manufacturing in the Arab sector, particularly after the outbreak of the war."[23] The Arab sector, then, accepted Jewish products; this aided the development of Jewish manufacturing by broadening the market. Although marginal, Arab purchases were nonetheless important. Indeed, a major study on the role of manufactuing concluded:

> It was by providing markets for manufacturers, rather than by supplying agricultural produce, that the existence of the local Arab sector can be said to have made possible the high share of manufacturing in the Jewish sector, especially in the period in which . . . Palestinian manufacturing was experiencing its most rapid growth. . . .[24]

Exchange between the Jewish and Arab sectors occurred mostly in or near the cities. Arab wholesalers seem to have played a rather significant role in Palestine's distribution system, a fact which became evident in 1936 when hostilities heightened. Many Jewish merchants depended upon Arab middlemen and suppliers, thus creating a certain vulnerability when the unofficial boycotts began. "As a result Jewish merchants attempted to become independent of the Arab trader."[25] In addition to wholesaling, intersectoral urban retail trade also occurred.

> Even during a year of riots some Jewish-owned stores had some Arab patronage. Based on sales experience in 1936, about 25 per cent of the more than 5,000 retail stores reporting had mixed clientele. In the cities of mixed populations such as Haifa and Jerusalem, the percentages were 43 and 39, respectively, compared with 15 in Tel Aviv. Clothing, building materials, machinery, and automobiles were the chief articles sold to the Arab trade.[26]

Again, it is obvious that intersectoral trade, although artificially constrained, was nevertheless significant.

One final factor relating to the Palestinian economy in general and to foreign trade in particular, merits note. This concerns Palestine's potential for transit earnings. Writing in 1938, Horowitz and Hinden expressed great hope in this regard.

> External transport is destined to become one of Palestine's great industries. As the key to both the land and the air routes to the East, Palestine has a particularly valuable geographical situation. Haifa is well placed for the vast hinterland of Syria, Iraq, and Iran and on the basis of this position, it has developed a transit trade of steadily growing dimensions.[27]

Nine years later another study was able to concur:

> There is general agreement that Palestine has enormous possibilities for the development of commerce and that it has, during the last decade or so, begun to be restored to its historic position as a center of trade between continents. The development of land, sea and air transportation moving from East to West and North to South is making Palestine an entrepot of great importance in the Middle East.[28]

World War II had a very significant impact upon the Palestinian economy. Comprehensive exchange control was almost immediately instituted. The physical volume of imports declined sharply, with decreases being concentrated in manufactured items. "It was the shutting off of these manufactured goods that gave Palestinian industry its great opportunity to capture the home market."[29] Despite difficulties in obtaining some raw materials, manufacturing activities expanded under this artificial stimulus. Military contracts provided a further stimulus. "By 1944," however, "the impetus which the war had given . . . was spent. In the following years the absolute growth of manufacturing was checked. . . ."[30]

The war also significantly altered trade patterns. The Middle East, which had previously supplied just under 20 percent of total imports, increased its share to 50 percent by 1944.[31] There was a corresponding shift in export destinations. During the 1936–39 period, the Middle East accounted for only 12.1 percent of exports; this figure rose to 65 percent in 1941 and 1943, decreasing to 55.8 percent in 1944. The war greatly disrupted citrus exports, this being the major reason why Europe, which had previously provided a market for over 80 percent of Palestinian products, barely accounted for 15 percent in 1944. Finally, petroleum from Iraq had traditionally been imported, both for domestic use and as a transit item. The completion of the Haifa refinery, however, allowed processing and refined oil export, this source earning approximately one-third of total export revenues in 1944.[32]

In summary, the economy was essentially divided into two sectors—Jewish and Arab. Economic intercourse was highly constrained; however, intersectoral trade did occur in areas in which mutual advantage was greatest. In additon, it is obvious that major economic benefits for both groups were foregone by the relative isolation from each other. It has also been shown that the economy was extremely dependent upon foreign trade and that other Middle Eastern countries normally provided Palestine with one-fifth of its imports while providing a market for roughly one-eighth of its exports. The Middle East, then, while not the major trading partner, was nevertheless making important contributions to the economy, particulaty in terms of supplies.

These latter facts should suffice to dispel the myth that the boycott does little harm because the Arabs have (or had) nothing to trade. Suprisingly, this error was committed in one of the few analytical treatments of Arab boycott, the author writing that during "the initial stages of the boycott period the Arab League had little to withhold . . . so direct sanction would be largely ineffective."[33] Later it is claimed that the Arab states were not trading with Israel, not only due to political antagonisms, "but also because there was simply so little to trade."[34] Such allegations not only ignore the principle of comparative advantage, which suggests that voluntary trade will be mutually beneficial even between poor countries, but they also ignore the historical facts. Trade did occur prior to the formation of Israel, and the Middle East was not an insignificant supply source. As a market for Palestinian exports, surrounding nations were of lesser importance, but a source of export earnings nonetheless.

The Boycott Mechanism

The Arab states[35]—despite even recent diplomatic moves— refuse to have any commercial dealings with Israel. In addition, all overland and pipeline transport routes to and from Israel have been severed. Neither Arab ports nor airfields may be used by carriers whose cargo is Israeli or whose destination is Israel. In addition, diplomatic representation and pressures have been placed upon other countries to induce them to sever their trade with Israel. Trade agreements entered into by Arab nations contain clauses prohibiting trade partners from reexporting Arab goods to Israel, and also prohibiting the export to an Arab country of any Israeli products or goods manufactured from raw materials of Israeli origin. These efforts have generally met with significant success in non-Arab Muslim states but have had only moderate influence on a national scale in other countries. Without question, the boycott has limited Israel's trade with Asia and Africa somewhat, although just how much is a moot question.[36] Nevertheless, whatever the boycott's success in the geographic areas, the total impact is marginal since these states are neither major Israeli suppliers nor markets (for reasons unrelated to the boycott).

Of greater significance are the measures taken against individual firms to induce a cessation of their Israeli trade. The Central

Boycott Office was established in Damascus, and national offices now function in each League state. The list of offenses that might result in blacklisting has increased considerably over the years, so that almost any commericial transaction can be deemed boycottable if the Arabs so choose. As a rule, however, the simple sale of consumer goods will not result in blacklisting since it is felt that such sales will aggravate Israel's balance of payments difficulties. "Investment, granting a patent license, providing technical aid, and supporting Israel in any way are the most common reasons for blacklisting."[37] Nevertheless, at least 70 major American firms do business with both the Arab states and Israel. The line between what is and what is not allowed is a thin and constantly changing one. For example, for a number of years the Ford Motor Company sold automobiles to Israel as well as Arab states; however, when the firm in mid-1966 began negotiating with its Israeli dealer for the assembly of trucks and tractors, the Boycott Committee voted to impose sanctions. Although considerable delay occurred in the implementation of this decision, Ford's Middle Eastern sales progressively decreased. In several Arab states there was a corresponding increase in Chrysler's sales.

Interestingly, many Japanese firms have refused to deal with Israel for fear of contravening boycott regulations; however, most would have been exempt due to the allowance for normal commercial transactions dealing in finished consumer goods. Nevertheless, the fear of offending the Arabs and losing Middle Eastern sales appears to have significantly depressed Japan's trade with Israel, particularly in terms of Japanese supplies.[38]

The blacklisting process is a complex and confusing one. Firms blacklisted by the Central Boycott Office in Damascus are supposed to appear upon the various national lists, but gaps and delays often occur. Generally, businesses are first warned of the imminence of their being blacklisted and given a period of time in which to cease their "improper" activities. Frequently this time period is extended and the Arabs are accommodating; on other occasions blacklisting is swift and even irreversible. A detailed study of boycott practices reveals little consistency in decision making; boycott operations are characterized by a high degree of arbitrariness and unpredictability.[39] Moreover, although strict penalties exist for boycott violators in Arab lands, and, as an inducement for boycott enforcement, 50 percent of the value of confiscated goods generally goes to customs and other officials discovering violations, there is evidence of considerable boycott contravention.[40] If the goods of blacklisted firms are needed and substitutes not available, the products tend to be purchased despite the blacklist.

Over the years boycott enforcement has become more efficacious. The pressures and counterpressures of boycott activities are clearly reflected in the Coca-Cola case. Early in April 1966 Coca-Cola refused a franchise to an Israeli bottling firm (Israel's largest). Despite the company's official statement that its decision was based upon "economic and market conditions rather than political,"[41] a storm of American protests—charging cowardice in the face of Arab threats—followed in the wake of the decision. One week later, in the midst of great controversy and under pressure from several domestic groups, Coca-Cola announced the granting of an Israeli franchise to an American banker. The company was then given three months by the Central Boycott Office to explain its decision. Despite negotiations, blacklisting became imminent. Coca-Cola sales began to fall before the boycott was actually implemented. The result has been that sales through independent, authorized bottlers have ceased. In short, the company has lost its Arab market, a rather substantial one.

Not only have foreign businesses lost Arab customers, but non-Arab customers may also be involved. This results from the secondary boycott, which proscribes Arab dealings with firms having commercial relations with blacklisted businesses. As a case in point, one concern surveyed by this writer was blacklisted by the Arab states for business dealings with Israel; however, this organization had neither Arab customers nor sources of supply and therefore apparently had little to lose from being blacklisted. Nevertheless, one of its customers—its major customer, in fact—did have considerable Arab dealings and was subject to substantial losses if it did not cease its ties with the blacklisted firm (or get the blacklisted firm to terminate its Israeli trade). When the blacklisted firm refused to comply, it lost its major customer, resulting in a 40–50 percent drop in its normal sales. By means of a secondary boycott, then, the scope of Arab economic sanctions is greatly increased.

The extension of the boycott to companies owned or operated by

Jews has also greatly expanded the economic consequences of Arab efforts. This extension is relatively new. The Arabs have always maintained that they are not anti-Jewish, but simply anti-Zionist. The League's Alexandria Protocol of 1944 reads as follows:

> The Committee deplores the horror and suffering which the Jews of Europe have endured at the hands of certain dictatorial states . . . but the question of these Jews must not be confounded with Zionism, for nothing could be more unjust than to settle the plight of European Jewry by another injustice at the expense of the Palestinian Arabs.[42]

The anti-Israel campaign has taken on an anti-Semitic character because the establishment and promulgation of the state of Israel was, in large part, due to the financial contributions of world Jewry. Arab sentiments in this regard are clearly demonstrated by a remark made by King Faisal of Saudi Arabia: "Unfortunately Jews support Israel and we consider those who provided assistance to our enemies as our own enemies."[43] Thus, the economic ties between Israel and world Jewry have resulted in an extension of the boycott, making its economic consequences that much broader in scope.

A rather well-publicized example of the success of boycott intimidation efforts is the Mancroft affair. Lord Mancroft, an English Jew, was forced to resign his position with a British insurance company Norwich Union Insurance Societies, which faced the prospect of losing its large volume of Arab business if it did not comply with Arab pressures. However, when the English public became aware of the circumstances surrounding the resignation many angry policyholders cancelled and much business was lost anyway. There are dangers, then, in compliance as well as noncompliance.

The exact number of firms that have been boycotted is not known, while the total on any current list tends to vary due to continuous additions and deletions. "Firms on the boycott list totalled 605 as of December 1, 1963, including 167 U.S. firms."[44] of which 53 had been on for three years or more. "During 1965 more than 300 firms from 33 different countries were added to the blacklist."[45] The list has grown over the years. By 1976 there were more than 1,500 American firms and individuals alone being blacklisted. Furthermore, all subsidiaries and licensees are also blacklisted. For example, when Kaiser Industries was boycotted in 1965, 26 subsidiaries were specified as well. When Monsanto Chemical Company was listed, 40 related companies and subdivisions were itemized. Some blacklisted firms have changed their names in order to escape the boycott; however, several have been detected and the new company name as well as the old are then on the list. Since 1965 the United States Department of Commerce has requested notification of any and all requests to American exporters concerning restrictive trade practices, particularly pertaining to boycotts. A summary of the notifications indicates the scope of the boycott's activities.

In 1967 firms reported 7,929 transactions in which their co-operation in restrictive trade practices was requested. Nearly all of these involved restrictions by Arab countries against Israel. The principal types of restrictions reported were requests for certification that: the goods were not of Israeli origin (66%); the carrying vessel was not blacklisted (5%); and West German reparations to Israel were not involved (1%). Also included were some 19 questionnaires concerning the exporter's subsidiaries and financial interests in Israel.

From October 7, 1965, when the reporting requirement became effective, to the end of 1967, the Department had received reports covering a total of 14,228 transactions.[46]

During 1968 U.S. firms reported 6,805 transactions in which cooperation in restrictive trade practices, almost all against Insrael, was requested.[47] For 1969 the corresponding figure was 7,174 transactions.[48] Since the upsurge in oil prices that began in late 1973, the number of boycott requests and the general vigor of the boycott has increased substantially. For a three-month period in the spring of 1976, for example, 131 American banks alone "reported they had engaged in 8,026 transactions involving 14,392 requests to enforce restrictive trade practices."[49]

The boycott's impact with respect to shipping merits special note. Literally hundreds of ship were blacklisted over the years. Interestingly, either individual vessels or entire fleet operations are subject to blacklisting, so that it is possible for a company serving Israel to still serve Arab states as long as that company does not attempt to service Arab lands with a blacklisted vessel. It was disclosed in early 1960 that the United States government was in effect respecting the boycott through the U.S. Navy's "Haifa clause." Inserted into Navy contracts with oil tankers was an optional clause authorizing the Navy to cancel its charter if the carrying vessel were denied access to an Arab port because of previous trade with Israel. This clause had been made necessary due to a charter vessel's being forbidden to load oil in Saudi Arabia in 1957. Since the vessel was therefore not capable of rendering the necessary service, the Navy cancelled its contract. A lawsuit for breach of contract damages then followed. The Haifa clause was inserted to avoid this kind of situation and therefore save American taxpayers' money. However, the clause discriminated against those carriers having done business with Israel. This practice was officially terminated in 1960. A similar situation has probably prevailed in the transport of P.L. 480 agricultural surpluses to Arab lands. The U.S. Army Corps of Engineers has also abided by the boycott by excluding Jewish personnel from projects in Saudi Arabia.

Undoubtedly, one of the League's most successful weapons in the past was the blockade of the Suez Canal to Israeli shipping or Israel-related cargoes. Shortly after Egypt assumed control over the canal she repudiated Israel's right of access to that channel. For a time after the 1956 war, Dag Hammarskjöld secured permission for the passage of Israeli cargoes in non-Israeli ships. "Early in 1959 Egypt blocked even this limited form of transport beneficial to Israel,"[50] but after laborious negotiations prodded by Mr. Hammarskjöld, a new agreement was finally reached. By the end of 1959 the new understanding had been twice tested—by one Greek and one Danish vessel, each carrying cargoes consigned to Israel. Both ships were detained and their cargoes seized.

Egypt for eight years also blockaded the Gulf of Aqaba, at the southern tip of Israel, thus choking off potential Israeli trade to the East and retarding the development of the port of Eilat. In 1956, however, the Sinai Campaign cleared away the Egyptian garrisons commanding the Straits of Tiran, which gave entrance to the Gulf of Aqaba from the Red Sea, and the port became a major avenue of Israel trade. The 1967 Middle East war, of course, directly centered about this vital area.

Economic Impact

The degree of enforcement must be examined in assessing the amount of economic damage resulting from the boycott. It is here that an obvious weakness appears, for its application is very uneven. Zeal in such efforts often varies with domestic political pressures, intra-League politics, or with the existing economic circumstances in each particular Arab state. Decisions made by the Central Boycott Office must be passed on to the various national offices. Each boycott order is then published in the member states' official gazettes before becoming law. Finally, enforcement is implemented by the local offices.

The problems of enforcement essentially derive from the nature of the boycott mechanism itself. Both economic theory and practice suggest that collusive selling arrangements have a tendency to break down—both due to the inability to detect secret cheating, or if detected, to do anything to stop it—as the number of sellers increases. Secret cheating under the boycott—a collusive buying as well as selling arrangement—is just as likely. The mutually beneficial nature of voluntary trade is clearly brought out in this regard. With voluntary exchange, both parties benefit and the cessation of trade generally entails a loss to each. Since the incidence of this loss is uneven and each of the various Arab states have varying needs and differing degrees of antagonism against Israel, the potential for cheating is obvious. One report suggests that

> although the rules are clearly stated, their application varies. For one thing, Arab nations don't always agree on what constitutes a violation. Some businessmen suggest that the criterion is how badly certain products or services are needed by the Arab country in question.[51]

There are a variety of ways the enforcing states may contravene boycott rules. Examples include delayed timing of blacklisting or boycott implementation in the various Arab states, overt contravention (coupled with lax enforcement) when products of blacklisted firms are needed, "official transactions" and "normal commercial relations" loopholes, and finally, conveniently narrow interpretations of boycottable offenses as the need arises. In addition, there is even evidence of some direct exchange—by smuggling, false invoicing, and like methods—between Israel and its Arab neighbors.[52] It is, therefore, obvious that economic sanctions can rarely be imposed upon other states without a reciprocal impact. The costs to Zambia of its trade cessations with Rhodesia are a classic case in point. Although less obvious, there is little question that the Arab states themselves have suffered, in varying degrees, due to boycott activities.[53]

In attempting to assess the degree of economic damage inflicted by the boycott, the effectiveness of the blacklisting technique is a major concern. Unfortunately, no definitive results have been, or are likely to be discovered. This writer's 1969 survey found that roughly 50 percent of the firms blacklisted experienced no sales declines, the major reason being that the firms had little, if any, dealings with Arab peoples. It is, however, to be noted that the survey concentrated upon American firms; had more businesses of other nations been included, it is probable that more firms would have felt an impact. Of the firms affected, the majority lost Arab patronage, often as much as 50 percent or more of their Arab sales. Non-Arab patronage lost proved to be an infrequent occurrence. The size of the losses, however, varied, from negligible (with many Arab sales continuing) to complete. However, two of the four respondents who were pressured by the secondary boycott reported losing more than 50 percent of their non-Arab sales, while a third firm lost 25–50 percent. Although not specified, it is probable that in each instance one or two major customers abandoned their former suppliers due to Arab pressures.

It is probably safe to conclude that small firms are more susceptible to boycott pressures than larger ones. This is true because a majority if not all of their sales may be with Arab peoples or with one or two major non-Arab customers who might be vulnerable to Arab economic sanctions. In addition, it is unlikely that any great public outcry will be heard if a small firm complies with the boycott. Indeed, few people will probably ever find out. However, large international corporations are more in the public eye and more sensitive to the possible adverse publicity which compliance may evoke. Both Coca-Cola and Renault are good cases in point. In addition, with much greater diversity in their sales territories, the loss of the Arab market may be offset by sales elsewhere.

The statistical findings and the added comments of respondents clearly indicate the unevenness of the boycott and its frequent failure as well as its extreme potency. It should, however, be mentioned that some firms reporting no losses—due to the absence of Arab patronage—stated that they had anticipated entering the Arab market, some even having licensed Arab distributors; however, due to blacklisting these potential sales were never realized.

As to how the firms surveyed weighed the overall impact of Arab blacklisting upon normal operations, a little more than 57 percent stated that it had no effect, these essentially being the firms with little, if any, Arab patronage or whose extra Israeli sales cancelled the Arab losses. About 20 percent rated the overall impact as insignificant, with only mild changes having to be taken in company policies and operations, while roughly 15 percent experienced either moderately or highly significant effects. For these firms, the boycott was definitely disruptive, in a few cases extremely so.[54]

Mention should also be made of Israeli countermeasures. In January 1965 it was announced that the products of firms complying with Arab demands were to be subject to discriminatory treatment in Israel. In addition, early in 1966 Israel warned seven companies to stop doing business through third parties (to avoid conflict with the Arabs) or through dummy organizations—all seven acceded. Of course, the former measure will probably have little impact since firms complying with the boycott have by their very acts of compliance abandoned the Israeli market. The second measure will be more effective, but taken only slowly as Israel feels its market can match that of the Arabs. For years Israel has been aware of trade through intermediaries and has not interfered simply because of reluctance to force suppliers to choose between the two markets. Of considerably greater significance, however, have been the efforts of various domestic groups in non-Arab nations that have aroused a negative public reaction against firms acceding or appearing to accede to the boycott.

To demonstrate that the boycott has been rather damaging to some firms does not, of course, prove that Israel has lost either customers or suppliers because of it. Most companies ceasing Israeli operations state that their business was not satisfactory or did not match their expectations. It is rare than an organization admits to compliance. Hence, it is a moot question as to exactly how many companies have bowed to boycott pressure. Logic would suggest that some companies are more susceptible than others, and those with very heavy dependence upon Arab markets might be committing suicide by noncompliance. As one New York banker advised: "In some cases it would be a very good idea if the company with Middle Eastern markets didn't violate the boycott at all."[55]

The ability to withstand Arab economic pressure depends upon the size of the firm, both absolutely and relatively, the number of firms in the market, the actions and attitudes of competitors, and finally, the share of output that is marketed in Arab nations. In short, doing business with both the Arab states and Israel has been likened to walking on a tightrope, with a great deal of uncertainty prevailing.

Despite the difficulty in getting official confirmation of boycott compliance, several sources do report the actual termination of Israeli operations. *Business International* has written:

> There is no question that the boycott has hurt the sales of U.S. and European firms; many of them are winding up their business connections in Israel to get themselves delisted.[56]

Ellis reports: "Faced with the loss of their Arab markets, dozens of Western firms and shipping companies have capitulated to the boycott and severed trade ties with Israel."[57] Weigand confirms these findings, writing that it "is beyond dispute that many of these firms had to choose one market and forego the other."[58]

It is, therefore, quite clear that Israel has lost potential investment and trade opportunities and has also experienced cessations of existing commercial ties. A quantitative estimate of these impacts, however, is impossible. In part it is akin to the problem of measuring the height of a tariff. In order to measure the opportunity costs of unrealized potential trade it would be necessary to know first, how many firms cancelled Israeli-oriented plans (or decided not to plan in that direction at all), and second, what volume of trade these plans might have entailed. As for measuring direct losses rather than potential, the same thorny problem of the number of firms ceasing business is presented. This just cannot be known since the firms themselves will attempt to disguise the fact. One additional factor of importance exists. For each firm discouraged by the boycott—both potential and actual—it is likely that the void thereby created may be filled by other firms, thus reducing the original impact. If marketing opportunities appear promising to one business, it is likely that others will also be attracted. Similar firms may be similarly situated concerning their degrees of vulnerability to the boycott, but their responses may differ. Here then is another factor, essentially indeterminable, that would have to be known in order to make a meaningful estimate. The conclusion of the study in this area, then, is that on net balance Israel has undoubtedly experienced some absolute declines in trade ties and has foregone trade opportunities and potential capital inflows. The dollar value of these losses, however, cannot be estimated and may range from only very marginal losses to as much as hundreds of millions annually.

In what other areas has Israel been harmed by the boycott? Transportation costs have been the area of direct expense most affected. Israel is surrounded on every side (except the western portion facing the Mediterranean) by Arab land. Since all overland and pipeline transport methods are blocked, while at the same time the shortcut formerly provided by the Suez Canal is also denied, circuitous and lengthy trade routes have been used. This has increased freight and insurance costs and brought greater delays in supply arrivals. In addition, another factor tending to increase transport expenses is that vessels bound for (or leaving) Israel cannot load or unload at neighboring ports, meaning that they must frequently carry less than capacity cargoes.

Transport costs are also increased when items must be purchased from distant markets despite their availability in neighboring Arab lands. Perhaps the best example is petroleum. Crude oil has been brought by tanker to Haifa from all parts of the globe (most from Iran in recent years). Before 1948, however, the Haifa refinery received oil from Iraq Petroleum Company through pipeline. This form of transport, coupled with the relatively short distance involved, minimized freight charges. The pipeline had in the Mandate days carried oil to the Haifa port for export to Europe and other parts of the globe. Since 1948 this source of domestic fuel and export earnings has not existed. A Lebanese economist in 1967 stated the following with regard to the petroleum sanctions:

> With the boycott . . . Israel besides losing all the royalties, had had to expend some $300 million on a pipeline from Eilat

to Haifa, and it has had to pay $100 million for oil supplies (to
date) more than it would have had the pipeline from Kirkuk to
Haifa remained in operation.[59]

These figures seem reasonable despite the possible bias of
the source. The same situation prevails with several other products—essentially raw materials.

Israel has had consistent balance-of-payments deficits since its
founding, and extra transport costs arising from the boycott
contributed to the policy of creating an Israeli merchant marine.
Beginning with almost nothing in 1948—a few old ships that had
formerly brought Jewish immigrants illegally into Palestine—
Israel's tonnage in 1967 approximated 1.5 million. Most of this
was created through German reparations and produced in
West Germany. Now, however, Israel has its own shipyard.
Israelis often point to the development of their merchant
marine—of which they are quite proud—and state that this has
been one of the positive aspects of the boycott. However, given
Israel's factor endowments and price structure, it does not seem to
be an "economic" undertaking. Weigand concurs, stating:
"Although probably contrary to the law of comparative advantage,
the boycott encouraged Israel to develop its own fleet of ships."[60]
In short, the inputs directed toward the development and actual
operation of Israel's merchant marine would be of greater value
elsewhere. Hence, Israeli feelings concerning this development
may be likened somewhat to that of an underdeveloped country
proud of its new sports palace, despite the secondary economic
importance of the structure. Of course, the purpose—to conserve
hard currency earnings—has been served.

Another area of cost concerns the Haifa refinery. It was built to
process the oil coming to Palestine through pipeline, so that export
income in addition to transit fees would be earned. However,
because of the greater transport costs involved and because its
products are marketed only in Israel, the Haifa refinery for years
operated at far below capacity, for a long period at less than 50
percent. This underutilization has entailed costs that should be
recognized, although it seems that the needs of Israel's rapidly
growing economy have in recent years been able to utilize almost
fully the Haifa facilities.

An earlier section described the trade relationships between
Palestine and other Arab lands and the interactions between

Palestine's Jewish and Arab sectors. What would the present prospects for Israel in the Middle East be today? Without doubt, normal trade relations between Israel and her neighbors would result in greater savings and mutual advantage to all. Lacking raw materials and an abundance of natural resources, Israel could be expected to import considerable quantities of Arab exports. As Meyer suggests:

> Israel needs many of the raw materials currently produced in nearby Arab countries—cotton for her textile mills, cotton-seed meal for her fishponds, food grains for her bakeries, oil for her industry and motor transport. Today she buys most of these in the world's most expensive markets, while . . . sources lie tantalizingly near to her frontiers.[61]

Cattle fodder, meat, and hides are other likely imports. This is not to imply that Israeli trade would suddenly be centered on the Middle East; however, trade with the area—both imports and exports—could be expected to increase substantially.

Had Israel and the Arab nations been able to resolve their differences in the late 1940s, it could be expected that Israel would have shared in the benefits of intraregional trade. A United Nations report in 1963 noted that both Jordan and Lebanon sold more than 60 percent of their exports (computed on a value basis for the period 1957–62) to other Middle East nations. The corresponding figure for Israel was a mere 5.2 percent, this trade being exclusively with Cyprus and Turkey, that is, no reported trade between Israel and her Arab neighbors. Israel's imports from the Middle East were only 1.3 percent of her total imports; the corresponding figures for Jordan and Lebanon were 26.8 and 21.7 percent respectively.[62] These intra-Middle East trade statistics leave no doubt as to the potential interaction of Israel's economy with those of her neighbors, again assuming normal trade relations since 1948. The economic loss, then, can be viewed against this background of potential trade foregone.

It must be recognized that in the absence of trade all these years, new trade patterns could only be developed over time. It certainly could not be expected that Israel's participation in Middle Eastern trade would soon approximate its potential had normal relations always existed. In the beginning Israeli exports on the whole would continue to go to non-Arab markets, although the share of exports

to neighboring countries would be likely to increase steadily.
Recalling that Palestinian, essentially Jewish, manufacturing found
a market both with local Arabs and within the rest of the Middle
East, thus allowing for an expansion of Jewish manufacturing, such
markets could be reestablished were trade to be normalized. This
process, of course, would be gradual since many Israeli products
are relatively high priced and would have to compete with exports
of other nations. However, Israel's geographical proximity would
be a clear advantage.

Israel's imports from the Arab world could be expected to
increase substantially, particularly in terms of oil, bread grains, and
raw materials. On net balance, it appears that Israel might have an
adverse trade balance, with her neighbors. However, lower
transportation costs and the Arab supply of raw materials, food, and
petroleum would most certainly lower Israeli costs and enhance
her competitive position in other world markets. Many of the raw
materials imported would be processed and then exported, some in
all probability returning to the Middle East. Lower-priced imports
would also aid in reducing Israel's perennial inflation problems.

On the invisibles account, Israel would likely gain very
substantially. The opportunity cost of foregone service and
investment revenues has without question been very great. The
commercial potential of Palestine has not been realized in the state
of Israel; a Middle Eastern entrepôt has not emerged. Oil pipeline
royalties have been an important source of revenue for Syria,
Jordan, and Lebanon, and were a growing source for Palestine.
Similarly, the tolls on Jordanian and other Middle Eastern transit
trade would be very substantial, but have been foregone since
1948. It is also likely that Israel's thriving economy would attract
excess Arab capital. This has been channeled mainly through
Lebanese rather than Israeli brokers. In addition, many large
international businesses would have located their Middle East
headquarters in Israel—a former British Mandate and populated
by a highly literate, Western-oriented population. Instead,
regional offices of such firms are spread among the Arab countries.
Finally, as a growing entrepôt Israel would have been able to
attract much greater volumes of investment from the West. Many
of these opportunities foregone could still be realized if a true
peace were established.

During the Mandate period, Jewish services were exported to

both Palestinian Arabs and those in surrounding territories. These exports would also have grown considerably if normal commercial relations prevailed. Also, it is very likely that Israeli firms would be subcontracted by European businesses doing work in Arab countries. This potential for invisible earnings, even now, is likely to be considerable. Consequently, Israel's prospects for becoming a "Switzerland of the Middle East" were enormous; its progress toward this end, however, has been close to zero and remains stultified.

Boycott efforts have not only affected particular firms and certain non-League nations that have complied with boycott policies, but regional trade groups as well. This is particularly the case with the European Economic Community (EEC). Israel's trade, both exports and imports, is heavily concentrated with Europe. The very creation of the EEC and the subsequent reduction of intragroup trade impediments made the marketing of Israeli products more difficult. The special arrangements that France has with its former colonies accentuated these difficulties. The EEC is a vital market, and maintaining Israel's position has become one of its major economic and political tasks. For years Israel requested from the Common Market an associate-member status; the Arab states, however, applied tremendous pressure to prevent this.[63] The possibility of economic disruptions in Europe due to Arab retaliatory measures seemed to be a major hindrance to concessions for Israel. Here again, then, the Arab boycott worked to Israel's disadvantage. Jensen and Walter, in their Common Market study, report as follows:

> Problems encountered in the Israeli discussion, however, centered implicitly around the political repercussions of the Arab-Israeli conflict. Common Market negotiators seemed to fear vehement protests from the Arab nations, possibly even severance of diplomatic relations with EEC member-nations, if significant trade concessions were given to Israel.
>
> Early in March, 1964, moderate tariff and quota concescions were finally granted Israel by the EEC Council of Ministers. These concessions fell far short of the original Israeli request for full association with the EEC, but this latter objective was clearly inconsistent with the maintenance of reasonably cordial relations between the Common Market nations and the Arab countries.[64]

Other researchers also have documented both the necessity of maintaining Common Market trade ties and the enormous potential associate membership could bring.[65]

To the list of potential gains that are not realized because of Arab-Israeli antagonism must be added the advantages of joint irrigation projects, soil conservation, water desalinization, and antilocust schemes that would benefit both Arabs and Israelis. But these opportunities are either foregone or undertaken separately at high cost. Peace and normalized trade would also make joint tourist excursions to the whole of the Middle East feasible, thereby enhancing the foreign exchange receipts and general business in the entire region. In short, as one source suggests, the "economic costs of non-cooperation between the Arab states and Israel are staggering."[66]

Since Israel's economy has greatly depended upon unilateral transfers, it may be thought that Arab economic measures have had "boomerang" effects in the form of additional development funds and unilateral donations that Israel receives from world Jewry and other sympathetic parties—funds that might not otherwise have been forthcoming. If this hypothesis is correct, then to the extent that economic relations with the Arabs improved, less development funds would be forthcoming, thus diminishing the net gains from a resumption of normal trade. Indeed, it would indicate that a portion of the incidence of the boycott has been shifted to other parties. However, the facts do not bear out this supposition.[67]

The difficulties of making quantitative estimates of the costs of the boycott have been stressed. The value of opportunities foregone is impossible to ascertain. In all probability, these have been greater than the direct costs—increased transport expense, higher priced raw materials, and so forth. Two rather outdated estimates will be mentioned, although neither source discussed the method of calculation. Gardner Patterson, in a report to the U.S. State Department in 1953, estimated the annual cost of the boycott at $25–30 million.[68] Harry Ellis, in a 1957 publication, provided an estimate of roughly $40 million annually.[69] This latter figure probably underestimates the direct cost in the 1960s.

A reasonable conclusion concerning the boycott is that it has been an encumbrance often painful and prohibitive of certain actions, but one that has not had the lethal effect intended. Israel remains an economically viable nation and has enjoyed very rapid growth and development. Without the boycott, of course, its development (and that of its neighbors) would have been even greater. In short, the boycott's direct costs function more as a thorn in Israel's side. Concerning the indirect costs—the unrealized benefits of foreign investment, transit earnings, new manufacturing markets, joint Middle East ventures, and the gamut of opportunity costs enumerated earlier—the boycott has kept Israel from achieving its full economic potential. Such opportunities foregone are unquestionably considerable.[70]

Post-1967

An examination of economic sanctions is essentially a speculative exercise—a comparison of what is with what might have been. Therefore, it is in the nature of the subject that hypotheses and conclusions are rarely capable of empirical testing. However, the Six-Day War of 1967 provided—through Israeli conquest of additional areas—some empirical evidence to verify the previous analysis.

Economic linkages with the occupied areas has been and is occurring on the basis predicted. As in the Mandate period, trade has been artificially constrained. The increase in guerrilla activities as well as a fear of collaborator labels has no doubt served to keep commercial intercourse far below its optimum levels. The pattern of exchange mirrors that which existed under the Mandate. As of May 1968 it could be reported that roughly 90 percent of the West Bank's (occupied Jordan) agricultural surpluses (output in excess of local consumption) were being sold to its traditional markets in Jordan (and from there to other areas of the Arab world, as in the past). Ten percent of these surpluses have gone to Israeli industry, particularly for fruit and vegetable processing and canning, or to Israelis purchasing at open markets, or to export markets with transit through Israel.[71] West Bank exports to traditional markets, then, have been maintained, although importing from former sources is now more restricted. The direction of export trade—from the West Bank across Israel to the Mediterranean—clearly reflects the natural transit advantages that

Israel possesses. Interestingly, unmarked Israeli goods have entered the West Bank and from there have been reexported to the Arab world. In addition, Arab produce, "officially destined for the West Bank, found its way to the Tel-Aviv markets."[72]

By the end of 1968 higher Israeli wages and job opportunities had attracted more than 15,000 Arab workers in the occupied areas to employment in Israel. Arab labor has made particular contributions in agriculture, building trades, and tourism. In addition, by 1969 about 3,000 West Bank Arabs were employed by Israeli Arabs.[73] Inflationary pressures on wages have thus been eased. This free (actually work permits are given by Israeli authorities) movement of factors has been highly beneficial to each economy, but again is constrained by dislike of Israel and fear of reprisals from intense Arab nationalists.

Again reminiscent of the Mandate period, Israel's exports to the West Bank—a market which is becoming increasingly important to Israeli businessmen—consist largely of manufactured items and services. The West Bank economy has been booming and its growth, as a rule, had occurred without direct Israeli investments. In addition to agricultural innovations introduced by Israeli technicians, the stimulus for increased economic activities derives essentially from access to Israeli markets and from subcontracting revenues from Israeli firms, especially in textiles, furniture, woodworking, and related trades—areas of traditional Arab skill and advantage.

The 1968 volume of trade with the West Bank appears to have yielded Israeli exports of £280 million and imports from that area of roughly £230 million. A 1968 summary of trade with the occupied areas indicated these positive effects.

> The link with the occupied areas has proved extremely beneficial to the Israeli economy. . . . In particular it has helped to maintain the stability of prices and wages . . . the supplies of cheap Arab goods and services (vegetables, building stone, etc.) and helped to keep prices down in Israel.[74]

The reuniting of the two sections of Jerusalem (formerly it was not possible to pass from one sector to another) proved to be a boon to the tourist trade. Israeli capital has been invested in hotels and tourist facilities in the former Jordanian part of the city. As anticipated, 1968 and 1969 were record tourist years in terms of the number of tourists visiting, their length of stay, money expenditures, and a host of other indicators. In view of the tremendous tensions in the area and the guerrilla activities that have extended even beyond the Middle East, this tourist boom was even more remarkable.[75] Since the October 1973 war, however, Israel's tourist trade has waned considerably.

The 1970s have witnessed continued economic integration, despite the rising tide of Arab nationalism within the occupied areas. Since 1970, agriculture output in these areas has expanded very considerably. These increased crops have enabled substantial growth in exports. Figure 3 clearly illustrates the growing use of Israeli ports for the export of Arab production (industrial and agricultural) within the occupied areas.

A well-known economic axiom holds that the smaller the participating economy, the greater the relative benefits from trade. In short, although both economically large and economically small nations will benefit from trading with each other, the gains are most important to the smaller economic entities within whose boundaries there is less specialization and a more limited scale of market. Trade between Israel and the occupied areas is mutually beneficial but has a substantially greater impact upon the latter. Table 4 shows the remarkable economic growth that occurred in the West Bank and the Gaza Strip from 1968–73. It is to be noted that the 13.5 percent annual rate of growth in gross national product for these combined areas has already been adjusted for rising prices and population increases. Such rates of growth are highly exceptional and although they cannot be wholly attributed to trade ties with Israel, these ties undoubtedly are a major, probably *the* major, factor. In terms of exports, for example, the chief export is labor services provided by Arab employees to Israeli employers. "This item [labor service] which did not exist in 1967, gradually increased and reached $150 million in 1973,"[76] about half the occupied areas' total exports. The major products exported to Israel are agricultural. The primary imports from Israel are industrial goods. While the gains to Israel, a much larger economic entity, are not as great, the substantial impact upon Gaza and the West Bank reflects trade possibilities and the potential benefits. The potential benefits from expanded trade—and the costs of continued economic boycott—seem staggering when it is recalled

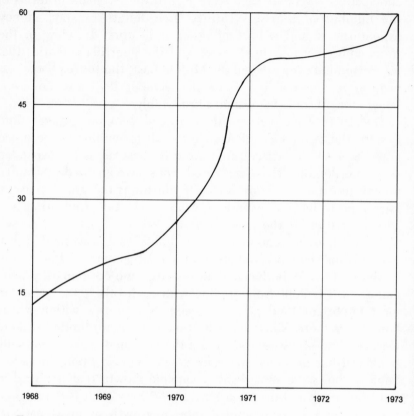

Fig. 3.   Exports from Israeli ports (air and sea)
Source: A. Lavine, ed., *Society of Change* (Jerusalem: Ministry of Social Welfare, 1974).

that there is still no direct trade with the remaining surrounding Arab lands or with other Arab League states.

Besides the already mentioned broad areas of exchange and basic comparative advantage, there are hundreds, even thousands, of individually minor, but aggregatively significant, areas of exchange that might emerge were trade instituted. The mutual interactions that are occurring in Jerusalem, where economic intercourse has advanced the most, give some indication of the scope of mutually advantageous exchange. More than 3,000 Arabs worked in the Jewish sector of the city by 1968, paying income taxes and enjoying the benefits of Israel's welfare system. Since that time a brisk traffic between the two sectors has emerged, both for business and pleasure. The Arabs have demonstrated a hearty demand for a

TABLE 4

Gross National Product in the West Bank and the Gaza Strip: 1968–73

(in 1971 prices)

	Gross National Product (million $)			GNP per Capita ($)		
	West Bank	Gaza Strip	Total	West Bank	Gaza Strip	Population Weighted Total
1968	120	50	170	200	130	180
1969	150	55	205	250	150	210
1970	165	70	235	270	190	240
1971	200	80	280	320	220	280
1972	250	100	350	395	260	345
1973	235	115	350	365	285	335
Annual rate of growth	14.5%	19.4%	16.0%	11.8%	17.0%	13.5%

Source: A. Lerner and H. Ben-Shahar, *The Economics of Efficiency and Growth* (Cambridge: Ballinger Publishing Company, 1975), p. 166.

wide variety of Jewish products and services (ice cream in
particular), while on Friday evenings Jewish youths often escape
the rigors of Sabbath closings by spending time in discotheques in
the Arab sector. These are only a few of the many individual minor
areas of exchange that have occurred but could hardly have been
predicted in a general theoretical analysis.

Since the October 1973 war and the soaring of petroleum prices,
Arab economic power has increased enormously. There can be no
question that the boycott of businesses dealing with Israel, or
third-party firms, has assumed new dimensions. Companies forced
to choose between the two frequently selected the more
prosperous Israeli market before 1973, but odds in these cases now
have substantially shifted against Israel.

Beginning in 1977, peace prospects for the Middle East
appeared to be on the verge of fulfillment. The year was also
historic with regard to economic events. In December *Business
Week* reported:

> No sooner had Egyptian President Anwar el-Sadat returned
> from his dramatic peace trip to Jerusalem than telex machines
> in Cairo began tapping out the first business proposals from
> Israel in 30 years.[77]

The gusto with which Israeli organizations—banks, publishing
houses, textile firms, chemical producers, tour promoters, and
others—greeted the prospects of peace and renewed trade is a
clear indication that Israelis assess the potential benefits as being
substantial. Another indicator is the position of the Israeli
government in negotiations, with its stress upon open borders and
normalized economic relations.

The second important development on the economic stage was
Egypt's proposed joint venture with Ford Motor Company and a
possible agreement with Coca-Cola. The Coca-Cola proposal,
announced in September 1977, is a $10 million joint venture to
develop 15,000 acres of citrus groves on presently arid land. The
agreement is contingent upon Coca-Cola's being removed from the
boycott list. Egypt, for its part, agreed to press for the company's
delisting. The agreement with Ford, however, which is expected
to require $145 million in initial investment and working capital, is
not contingent upon Ford's prior delisting. In response to this
Mohammed Mahgoub, head of the Arab League Boycott Office,

was quoted as saying: "Egypt has violated the boycott regulations and there isn't any justification for it."[78] He warned that vehicles and engines produced at the Egyptian facility would be banned elsewhere in the Arab world. There was even talk of boycotting all Egyptian products.

In early 1978 fourteen tainted, Israeli-grown oranges were found in Europe, and an Arab Palestinian group claimed responsibility for contaminating the fruit. In early February, after a Spanish orange injected with mercury was discovered in West Germany, the authorities there speculated that the Spanish fruit was mistaken for Israeli produce. These actions were clearly aimed at reducing Israel's exports and brought another dimension to the economic warfare.

Summary

The Arab boycott has been inimical to Israel's growth and development, despite unfounded protestations to the contrary.[79] Israel has incurred numerous extra expenses in terms of higher transport costs and more expensive raw materials. It has been denied the benefits of intraregional trade and has had its volume of international trade curtailed. The opportunity costs of the boycott—in terms of unrealized foreign capital inflows, lost business ties, a failure to jointly utilize the Jordan and Lintany (in Lebanon) rivers, foregone transit trade earnings, and related opportunities unrealized—have unquestionably been very substantial, although by their very nature they are essentially incapable of quantitative measurement. Arab boycott efforts indicate clearly the mutually beneficial nature of trade and the fact that sanctions cannot be imposed upon one nation without reciprocal impacts upon the boycott initiators. Finally, despite the boycott's effectiveness (in terms of imparting meaningful economic damage), it has been almost totally without political success. The aim of destroying Israel through economic sanctions has not been achieved. Israel's growth has been remarkable—due to a combination of many factors—despite the boycott. In its absence the development possibilities would be even greater.

5

Global Sanctions Against Rhodesia

Great Britain imposed political and economic sanctions against Rhodesia in the fall of 1965. Shortly thereafter, the United Nations also implemented voluntary sanctions—becoming mandatory a year later—and it was assumed by many observers that Rhodesia would soon be brought to its knees. The intended political results, though, never occurred. Instead, Rhodesia was able to withstand and adjust to sanctions.

Historical Background

Rhodesia is a landlocked territory approximately the size of California, bounded on the north and northwest by Zambia, on the south by South Africa, by Mozambique on the east and northeast, and by Botswana on the southwest (Figure 4). Salisbury, the capital, is the largest city, with Bulawayo being the second most populous town. The 1975 population was just over six million, of which some 273,000 (4+ percent) were white.

The Portuguese were the first Europeans to enter the area. The region's mineral potential made it attractive to outside powers, and both the British and the Portuguese later laid claims. By 1891 an Anglo-Portuguese agreement was signed that fixed the boundary with Mozambique and ended European antagonisms over the region. Colonization, under the auspices of the British South Africa Company, was begun, and thousands of white settlers arrived. Significant progress was made in the area of transport and communications, the railroad from the Portuguese city of Beira reaching Bulawayo in 1896 and Victoria Falls in 1904. Later, an outlet to the sea by railroad to the Cape was opened.

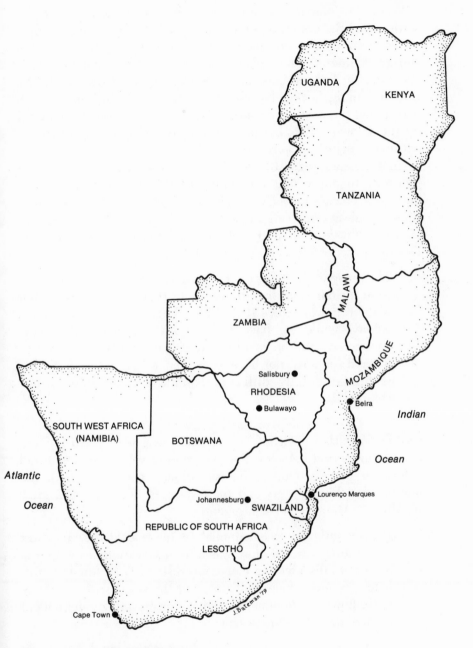

Fig. 4. Southern and Eastern Africa

When the company's original period of rule expired in 1914, the settlers had the option of either joining the Union of South Africa or continuing the company's charter pending the grant of self-government. They chose the latter. After World War I pressures for full self-government became quite strong. In 1922 a referendum again rejected incorporation into the Union of South Africa, and the next year Southern Rhodesia was formally annexed by the Crown.[1] This began its status as a self-governing colony within the British Empire.

An understanding of Rhodesia's historical autonomy is important in order to appreciate the political problems that led to the unilateral declaration of independence (UDI) in 1965. Southern Rhodesia always enjoyed a unique relationship to the Crown. Mr. Herbert Bowden, in a speech to the House of Commons on December 7, 1966, described the situation:

> The present problem goes back over many years during which time Britain has had the responsibility for Rhodesia but without power. Since 1923 when Rhodesia formally became a colony, while we have had certain constitutional powers connected with the government of that country, we have had no civil servants, nor have we had an army, on the spot. This is fundamentally different from the position in other colonies.[2]

"Close British control of this largely self-sufficient country . . . was never either welcome or strongly asserted."[3] During the thirty-year period between the inception of self-government and federation with two other British colonies (in 1953), both the number of white settlers and their spirit of independence grew steadily. As Margery Perham suggests,

> British authority was minimal in internal affairs. Its most important manifestation was the reservation for imperial assent of bills affecting native interests. . . . In Rhodesia this veto was never once used. . . . But the very existence of this curb, however nominal, chafed the increasingly independent spirit of the white Rhodesians. . . .[4]

A tradition of self-government by whites evolved with only slight interference from Britain. In this situation, Europeans had a privileged political and economic status. Indeed, the Lands

Apportionment Acts of 1936 and 1941 allocated only 50,000 square miles to the more than 2.5 million Africans, while 75,000 square miles of economically superior land was allotted to 215,000 white settlers. Occasionally, though, the Commonwealth's concern for the rights and humanitarian treatment of natives was expressed. In 1929 the British government issued statements asserting essential political and economic rights of Africans and proposed that Africans should ultimately share in the government of their territories.[5] While these "Black Papers," as they were called by the white settlers, dealt specifically with the more central regions, whites in the Rhodesias were upset. Their response was to suggest that Rhodesia and Northern Rhodesia (more directly controlled by the Crown) merge to defend against the forces threatening them. In 1939, however, Whitehall vetoed the proposed union. This simply piqued Rhodesian desires for even greater autonomy and resulted in unceasing efforts by the settlers for a merger. In 1953 Britain agreed to a union of three territories, the two Rhodesias and Nyasaland, forming the Federation of Rhodesia and Nyasaland. Control effectively rested with the whites of Southern Rhodesia.

In retrospect it is difficult to imagine what expectations Britain could have had concerning the permanence of the Federation. Racial problems were bound to create serious, although perhaps not unsolvable, difficulties. A system of dual voting roles maintained European political domination, with the Federation's pseudofranchised blacks witnessing the growth of African rule elsewhere on the continent. Further, despite the interdependence of the three territories, most development and industrial growth that occurred during federation years was concentrated in Southern Rhodesia. Hence, unequal participation both in political processes and economic development led to increasing African dissatisfaction, particularly among the emerging African leadership. Local African leaders pressed for establishing the "one man, one vote" principle. Whites, fearing that such an enactment threatened their positions, wealth, and, perhaps, their very lives, became increasingly intransigent. After the federal elections of 1958, tensions were high; widespread rioting broke out in early 1959. The Federation was formally dissolved at the end of 1963, with Nyasaland later becoming the independent state of Malawi, Northern Rhodesia becoming the independent state of Zambia, and Rhodesia maintaining its traditional status within the British

Commonwealth. Despite the political breakup, certain common services and economic activities endured.

Negotiations for a new Rhodesian constitution had begun far in advance of the Federation's official dissolution. In 1961 a new constitution was approved by the (largely white) electorate. The Rhodesians considered this a major step toward independence, although the British, despite a further limitation of their effective power, did not deem it to be "an independence constitution."[6] After the failure of the Federation, Rhodesia further pressured Britain for independence. Negotiations dragged on for two years, the crucial issue being British insistence that firm guarantees of progress toward African majority-rule be given before independence could be granted.

The Presanctions Economy—An Overview

The expanding Rhodesian mining industry created a population influx during the first two decades of the 1900s that in turn produced a significant demand for a wide variety of products, particularly food and related consumer goods. Farming developed as a major economic activity, with most other commercial undertakings becoming centered in Bulawayo and Salisbury. Economic growth was considerable but ceased in the general stagnation of the 1930s.

Tobacco was introduced to Rhodesia in 1910 and soon became the major product in terms of value. Corn, however, was the pioneer crop and remains important as a product for local consumption, whereas tobacco is essentially for export. The cattle and dairy industries are also significant. In general, agriculture has been fairly diversified, although production for export historically has been concentrated in just a few crops. Most of the cash crops were and are grown by white farmers. A 1964 study reported the following:

> Self-sufficiency in sugar was achieved in 1962, and the growing of vegetables was encouraged by heavy duties on imports. Although there are periodic meat shortages in Southern Rhodesia, the colony is self-sufficient in milk and other dairy products. Citrus fruits are raised largely for the

local market, although some are exported. Peanuts are grown extensively by Africans.[7]

Before World War II there was little significant industrialization, primarily because of limited domestic demand and the availability of imports. The African majority constituted an economic minority whose livelihood was based upon subsistence agriculture that, for a variety of reasons, had tended to deteriorate. The outbreak of World War II, however, brought major changes.

> Goods previously imported became practically unavailable, thus creating demand for local industries; chrome and asbestos assumed strategic importance; world shortage of agricultural produce provided a rapidly growing outlet for farmers' output . . . an air training scheme was implemented in the country, in association with the British Government. . . . Imperial expenditure on the scheme alone almost equalled the indirect benefit which the country derived from its entire gold-mining industry.[8]

As the war-induced stimuli dissipated in the late 1940s, a new external force—world shortage of raw materials (coupled with the dollar shortage)—maintained high levels of domestic activity. "Tobacco in particular was greatly stimulated by the limitation on dollar expenditure by the United Kingdom. . . ."[9] Output tripled over the 1945–58 period. A further influx of Europeans occurred, buoying internal demand in general and construction activities in particular.

A significant urban manufacturing sector emerged by the 1950s, and this white, urban manufacturing class was a group somewhat distinct from the rural, white agriculturists who had previously dominated Rhodesia's power structure. At the same time, the demand for unskilled manufactuing labor increased. Africans usually filled these positions; however, the stability and reliability of African labor, particularly in urban employment, has been minimal (almost entirely owing to the persistence of tribal customs). The labor situation, along with several other factors, contributed to an increased demand for other inputs.

The sectoral origins of Rhodesian gross domestic product for 1954–64 are presented in Table 5. Agriculture continued to be the leading sector, followed by manufacturing, distribution, transport

TABLE 5

Industrial Origin of Rhodesian Gross Domestic Product

1954–64

(£ millions)

	1954	1955	1956	1957	1958	1959	1960	1961	1962	1963	1964
Agriculture	38.3	39.7	46.1	47.0	46.7	50.7	51.7	61.8	62.0	63.8	67.7
Mining and quarrying	14.5	15.7	16.7	17.5	17.6	17.2	19.1	18.7	17.0	15.8	16.9
Manufacturing	24.6	26.8	30.1	35.8	38.8	41.8	45.4	49.5	51.8	51.2	54.3
Building and construction	13.2	15.5	17.9	23.1	23.7	21.3	20.7	16.7	15.1	13.9	13.5
Electricity and water	4.0	4.6	5.5	6.4	6.8	7.3	10.4	12.2	12.3	13.2	13.7
Distribution	23.4	27.0	29.6	32.4	34.3	36.8	39.9	39.9	40.1	40.9	41.5
Banking, insurance, and finance	1.9	1.3	2.0	2.7	3.8	4.4	3.9	3.6	3.8	4.1	3.9
Real estate	3.1	3.7	4.3	5.4	6.2	6.3	6.7	6.5	7.0	6.6	7.1
Ownership of dwellings	4.8	5.4	6.4	7.1	7.9	8.3	8.6	9.4	9.8	10.3	10.4
Transport and communication	12.3	14.8	17.3	20.2	19.3	23.5	25.8	25.4	25.6	28.7	30.9
Public administration and defense	6.5	7.3	8.0	9.7	11.0	11.4	12.2	13.7	14.6	15.6	14.6
Education	3.3	3.8	4.3	5.5	6.1	6.9	7.6	9.0	9.9	10.6	11.0
Health	1.5	1.8	2.0	2.1	2.3	2.3	2.5	2.7	2.9	3.6	3.6
Domestic services	5.5	6.1	7.0	7.5	-8.1	8.5	8.9	9.4	9.8	10.1	10.5
African rural household services	2.6	2.7	2.8	2.8	2.8	2.9	3.2	3.3	3.2	3.9	4.2
Services, other	8.4	10.0	11.7	13.7	14.5	15.4	16.0	16.5	17.4	16.5	16.7
Gross Domestic Product	167.9	186.2	211.7	238.9	249.9	265.0	282.6	298.3	302.3	308.8	320.5

Source: *Standard Bank Review*, April 1966, p. 39

and communications, mining and quarrying. Tobacco was the main agricultural product, followed by meat, sugar, cotton, tea, and peanuts. The major subsistence crops were corn, millet, and sorghum. Industrial products included metals, food processing, textiles, clothing and footwear, beverages and tobacco, and chemicals. In the mining sector Rhodesia in 1965 was the world's third largest producer of asbestos as well as a significant producer of chrome ore. Gold, copper, coal, iron ore, and tin were also produced.

The Rhodesian economy, in short, was a relatively broad-based one. Although income per head in 1964 was only £76, this figure concealed more than it revealed because of inequality of income distribution. The economy has always been dual: along side a developed, monetized sector was one based on primitive agriculture. The economy, though, provided sufficient subsistence to permit (together with improved medical facilities and drugs) a population explosion. Less than 10 percent of the African population were employed as wage earners in the modern section. Within the monetized sector, though, the average productivity of employed whites was more than ten times the corresponding figure for Africans (taking no account of subsidized services for the latter). It is interesting that the average earnings of whites in Rhodesia were considerably higher than the corresponding incomes of whites in neighboring South Africa. A sharp color bar divides the industrial labor force. Skilled work is performed almost exclusively by whites, and unskilled by Africans. Africans do participate in semiskilled jobs, as do the remaining nonwhites. Despite the substantial growth in the economy's industrial base, few African workers have significantly improved their job status, mainly because the white unions have enforced "equal pay for equal work."

Giovanni Arrighi has suggested four categories of the Rhodesian political structure, all based upon the nation's economic substructure.[10] The first, representing international capital, is comprised of the managers of foreign corporations' subsidiaries, primarily engaged in the foreign trade sector. "In 1960 about half of total company profits earned in Rhodesia accrued to firms not domestically controlled. . . ."[11] Although significant economically, the political importance of the category—a group that had been seriously harmed by sanctions—has declined. A second category, representing domestic capital, consists of local entrepreneurs and businessmen, a class that developed rapidly during the Federation years in response to increased production of manufactured goods. Farmers are the third category, and their influence is considerable in spite of being less than 6 percent of the electorate. Category four encompasses employees and others, and they are the vast majority of white Rhodesians. Under the 1965 constitution this group is nominally the basic source of political power.

Table 6 provides a breakdown of African and non-African employees by sector in 1965.[12] The small number of non-Africans engaged in agriculture and mining (the chief export sectors) merits note, since these sectors are most directly susceptible to sanctions. Tobacco farmers and their employees (mainly Africans) have been particularly harmed by sanctions. The table indicates the numerical dominance of the Africans, which was about seven times that of the non-Africans. Their concentration in the export-related sectors—agriculture, manufacturing, and mining—suggests that Africans would bear much of the burden of sanctions.

TABLE 6
Non-African and African Employees in Rhodesia, 1965
(in thousands)

	Non-African	African
Agriculture and Mining	7.2	314.0
Manufacturing	16.0	68.9
Distribution	18.3	30.2
Transport	10.3	16.8
Public Sercies	18.1	48.9
Banking, Insurance, and Finance	6.0	2.0
Other	13.1	53.5
Totals	89.0	534.3

Source: T. Curtin and D. Murray, *Economic Sanctions and Rhodesia* (London: Institute of Economic Affairs, 1967), p. 19.

A unique characteristic of the African labor force in Rhodesia is that less than half has been indigenous, with the rest generally coming from surrounding areas. Dependence upon extraterritorial labor was so strong that the Rhodesian government at times provided free transport and other facilities to move workers and their families to and from needed employment centers. This African labor was actively sought until the 1960s when it had become redundant and the policy of recruiting workers was ended.

Although non-African unemployment rates have historically been extremely low, the rate of African unemployment, even before sanctions, posed an increasingly serious problem. A 1964 study pessimistically concluded that "Southern Rhodesia will face either a growing volume of urban African unemployment or a gradual deepening of poverty in the African peasant farming section."[13]

In studying the impact of sanctions, the role of international trade merits special attention. During the years of federation close to 50 percent of the Federation's exports went to the United Kingdom, with 6 percent to South Africa. Approximately 37 percent of total imports came from Britain, while South Africa provided about 34 percent.[14] With the dissolving of the Federation, many observers expected that Rhodesia would face balance-of-payments difficulties because of loss of markets in Zambia and Malawi; however, these markets remained significant and the visible trade balance was favorable. Exports in 1964 earned 38 percent of the national income, with 34 percent being spent on imports—both very high figures.[15] The commodity make up of exports is presented in Table 7. Most Rhodesian exports were raw materials, with the major item being tobacco (31 percent of the total value of exports in 1964). Mineral exports reached almost 22 percent. Individual items of importance in addition to tobacco were gold, copper, asbestos, sugar, apparel, and various manufactured goods. Table 8 provides a breakdown of Rhodesian imports. Machinery, transport equipment, chemicals, petroleum, foodstuffs, and miscellaneous manufactured items were the major imports. While a high proportion of imports were luxury manufactures, the importance of machinery, spare parts, and raw materials should not be discounted. Before March 1965 petroleum imports to Rhodesia were sufficient to serve the needs of both Rhodesia and Zambia.

Table 9 indicates the direction of Rhodesia's foreign trade for 1964. The United Kingdom was the major trading partner, providing 30.4 percent of Rhodesia's total imports, while absorbing 25.5 percent of all exports. The trade balance with Britain was adverse to Rhodesia by £5 million. South Africa was the second leading supplier, although as a customer it absorbed only 7.5 percent of total exports. The trade balance with South Africa was quite unfavorable. Zambia, on the other hand, purchased roughly one-fourth of Rhodesia's exports, with few offsetting Rhodesian

TABLE 7
Rhodesian Exports, 1964–65
(including gold sales)
(£,000)

	Jan.–Sept. 1964	Jan.–Sept. 1965	1964
Gold	5,285	5,041	7,086
Refined copper	2,976	4,105	3,552
Tin	396	390	565
Asbestos	7,160	7,050	10,015
Chrome ore	2,005	2,640	2,500
Coal	1,179	1,542	1,657
Ferro-chrome	1,418	1,266	1,833
Pig iron	2,134	2,067	2,550
Sugar	2,675	2,580	3,680
Tobacco	29,030	33,434	39,221
Maize	94	266	350
Wattle extract	349	428	724
Cattle hides	412	504	539
Meat (fresh, frozen and chilled)	2,369	3,013	2,992
Other meats	1,918	1,907	2,050
Cigarettes	1,264	1,023	1,765
Footwear	1,145	1,324	1,558
Apparel	4,022	4,374	5,422
Radios and parts	1,148	1,555	1,726
Motor cars and trucks	1,422	2,437	2,213
Tires and tubes	712	847	972
Ale, beer, and stout	319	611	461
Timber (rough, sawn, or machined	662	666	902
Lithium ore	436	304	543
Paints	425	357	551
Soap and detergents	687	723	953
Fabrics in the piece	842	1,044	1,175
Blankets	371	512	427
Steel ingots and billets	557	323	643
Steel bars	464	631	588
Copper bar and rod	776	298	956
Structural steel	651	533	1,029
Furniture (metal and wood)	434	631	588
All other commodities	17,706	24,256	24,815
	93,443	108,682	126,601

Source: *Standard Bank Review*, January 1966, p. 37.

TABLE 8
Rhodesian Imports, 1964–65
(£000)

	Jan.–Sept. 1964	Jan.–Sept. 1965	1964
Food	7,808	7,095	9,700
Beverages and tobacco:			
Unmanufactured	2,565	2,409	2,774
Other	689	555	961
Crude materials	3,928	3,704	5,467
Mineral fuels	4,657	4,299	6,187
Oils and fats	412	886	556
Chemicals	8,397	9,958	11,516
Manfactures classified by materials	21,134	24,073	28,063
Machinery and transport equipment	23,347	28,245	31,240
Miscellaneous manufactured articles	7,739	8,601	10,653
Miscellaneous transactions	1,880	2,091	2,578
Totals	82,556	91,916	109,695

Source: *Standard Bank Review*, January 1966, p. 37.

imports. The United States was a distant third as a supplying nation, and ranked seventh as an export market, following Zambia, the United Kingdom, South Africa, West Germany, Malawi, and Japan.

Typically, Rhodesia had deficits in the invisibles accounts, with

TABLE 9
Direction of Rhodesian Foreign Trade, 1964

Country	Exports to: (% of total)		Imports from: (% of total)	
United Kingdom	25.5		30.4	
South Africa	7.5		24.4	
Zambia	25.8		4.9	
United States	3.3		6.8	
West Germany	6.6		3.9	
Japan	4.7		4.0	
Malawi	4.7		1.5	
Others:	21.9		24.1	
Africa		4.2		2.2
Non-Africa		17.7		21.9
Total	100.0		100.0	

Source: Robert B. Sutcliffe, *Sanctions Against Rhodesia* (London: African Bureau, 1966), p. 3.

major deficits in transport expense and investment income. Tourism, on the other hand, had been an important earner of foreign exchange. Further, in 1964 the nation enjoyed a net inflow of long-term capital. "If 1964 is considered a normal year, then Rhodesia's pattern of international payments is seen to be very nearly in balance without the necessity for foreign loans or for running down the reserves."[16]

The economy continued to grow during 1965, the increases for both 1964 and 1965 being largely export-generated. That year (1965) also witnessed an increase in investment and a long overdue recovery in the building trades. Despite a decline in the agricultural sector, the gross domestic product rose from £328.0 million (1964) to £352.8 million in 1965.[17] To summarize, Rhodesia's economy by 1965 had emerged from a period of stagnation and was in the midst of a rather vigorous expansion. The economy was diversified and had a growing internal demand. Significantly, international trade played a major role in the economic advance. It is against this background that sanctions were first imposed.

Sanctions: Implementation and Compliance

The government of Harold Wilson came to power in Britain in the fall of 1964, and it reiterated earlier British opposition to Rhodesian independence. Perhaps anticipating unilateral action on the Rhodesians' part, Wilson, on October 27, 1964, declared that the decision to grant independence rested solely with Britain and its Parliament and that any declaration of independence by the Rhodesians would be illegal and constitute rebellion. Wilson enumerated five principles that had to be satisfied before independence would be granted:

1. guarantees of unimpeded progress toward majority rule, as already contained in the 1961 constitution;
2. guarantees against retrogressive amendment of the constitution;
3. immediate improvement of the political status of the African;
4. progress toward the cessation of racial discrimination;

5. acceptance of the proposed basis for independence by the people of Rhodesia as a whole

The subsequent curbing of activities and alleged "political oppression" of both whites and blacks who incited violence in opposition to the Rhodesian regime, later led to the addition of a sixth principle:

6. no oppression of the majority by the minority or vice versa, regardless of race.

Negotiations finally broke down, and the Rhodesian Prime Minister, Ian Smith, left London on October 11, 1965. One month later Rhodesia issued a unilateral declaration of independence (UDI).

This determination in the face of great pressure can best be understood in light of Rhodesian attitudes and fears concerning majority rule. It is this very determination that has so far maintained the Smith regime and Rhodesian morale despite a decade of economic sanctions and world opprobrium. The productive white minority, of course, resists most proposed changes in the status quo. More important, however, is the serious fear of losing perhaps everything for which they have worked. "It is the disorders, the rejection of democracy and the violent speeches of many African leaders that disgust, and to some extent alarm, many Rhodesian Europeans."[18] They view most of the new African states as traditional dictatorships in which both the rulers and the ruled happen to share the same skin color. Rhodesians were affronted by Britain's granting these areas independence long before they were ready, while at the same time denying it to Rhodesia, which had shown itself capable of self-government for so long. The prospects of majority rule—of African rule—strike horror in the minds of most Rhodesian whites. As Perham suggests:

Of all the negative lessons they draw from the stormy prospects to the north, none has been more horrifying than the events in the Congo. If to us the atrocities perpetrated in that country were almost unbearable to read, how much more dreadful they must have been to white people, themselves minorities in the heart of Negro Africa, who watched these bloodly events from a place not so many miles away and who saw some of the refugees from the terror arriving in their country.[19]

On November 16, 1965, shortly after the UDI, Britain imposed political and economic sanctions against Rhodesia, which included cessation of all British aid, removal of Rhodesia from the sterling area and Commonwealth preference system, and a ban on tobacco and sugar purchases. The day following UDI the United Nations Security Council met, condemned the unilateral action, and called upon all nations to withhold recognition and render Rhodesia no assistance. On November 20 the Council again convened, requesting all nations to break general economic relations with Rhodesia and specifying a petroleum embargo in particular. The first year U.N. sanctions were voluntary, the Security Council only requesting compliance. Neither these actions nor the intermittent negotiations between Britain and Rhodesia succeeded in settling the crisis. On December 16, 1966, for the first time in its history, the United Nations invoked mandatory economic sanctions, in accord with Articles 39 and 41 of its Charter. More specifically, imports of the following Rhodesian products were proscribed: asbestos, iron ore, chrome, pig iron, sugar, tobacco, copper, meat products, hides, skins, and leather goods. In addition, the supply of arms, aircraft, motor vehicles, and equipment for arms manufacture were also banned. Finally, supplying oil or aiding its transport to Rhodesia was prohibited. This inclusion had been urged by Great Britain, which emphasized repeatedly that it had no intention of resorting to arms to bring down the Smith regime.

Rhodesia was still independent of foreign influences and showed no signs of bowing to sanctions in May 1968, so in that month the Security Council banned the import of any and all Rhodesian goods by other nations. At the same time, the U.N. prohibited the sale and/or supply of any goods to Rhodesia (with the exception of medical supplies and humanitarian items). Specific mention was also made of states acting as ports of transit for goods destined to Rhodesia. All air transport to Rhodesia was prohibited and withdrawal of all consular and trade representation was specified. The Council also deplored and censured those nations not abiding by previous U.N. resolutions. Thus, voluntary sanctions gave way to mandatory selective sanctions and, finally, to mandatory comprehensive sanctions.

Despite this multitude of resolutions and declarations, considerable lags existed in the implementation and effective enforcement of the declared boycotts. Because sanctions were voluntary in the early stages, many member-states simply failed to comply. With compliance a part of an individual nation's policy, there was generally a time lag between the U.N. resolutions and the enabling legislation in member countries. Further, most domestic trade control enactments required future rather than immediate termination of trade. This typically referred only to new contracts and did not effect the implementation of preexisting agreements. In anticipation of possible sanctions, Rhodesian importers had tended to place larger than usual orders and to contract for longer than normal periods. Those regularly purchasing Rhodesian products did likewise. In this fashion enacting sanctions that exempted existing contracts delayed effective imposition of the embargo, even if the enabling legislation itself had been quickly passed.

Before the mandatory comprehensive sanctions, probably 60 percent of Rhodesian exports, but only 15 percent of normal imports, had been banned. In the case of the United States, which offered ready compliance, a virtual embargo on all exports to Rhodesia was not enacted until July 16, 1968. This order allowed twenty-one additional days to shipments already in transit or at ports of exit for Rhodesian delivery. Thus the lapse between initial sanctions (November 1965) and a total embargo by the United States covered a period of approximately thirty-three months. Further, in 1971–72 the U.S. Congress relaxed controls to allow mineral imports from Rhodesia. Finally, the effectiveness of the enforcing nations in policing their own trade controls is an important factor. Degrees of enforcement have varied considerably, yet after U.N. sanctions became mandatory and comprehensive, a tightening of trade flows to and from Rhodesia did become noticeable.

A more detailed examination of Rhodesia's trade is required for understanding the impact of sanctions. The United Kingdom, the major trade partner, took the lead in imposing sanctions, and by February 1966 an almost total ban on exports to Rhodesia was in force. Even earlier, approximately 95 percent of all British imports had been embargoed, with the remaining 5 percent, mainly manufactured items, also banned in February. In addition, there were financial curbs. All British aid ceased. Rhodesia was removed from the sterling area, denied access to the London capital market, and subjected to special exchange control restrictions. These measures froze major traditional sources of financing, although there were some temporary exceptions. All were aimed at reducing Rhodesia's ability to import. Pressures upon Switzerland also resulted in the blocking of a modest amount of reserves at the Swiss National Bank.

In general, the Rhodesian banking system was overlent against domestic deposits and relied on net borrowing from London. With British banking facilities prevented from providing the traditional credit, Rhodesian banks were forced to call in loans and tighten the money market considerably. The enforcement of tight money in Rhodesia, it was hoped, would result in a decrease in domestic investment. London anticipated that the tightening of credit would cause considerable Rhodesian discontent and perhaps call forth sufficient pressure upon Smith to negotiate a settlement. But if the Smith government, to avoid tight money, created credit itself, then it was expected that domestic inflation would result and, presumably, arouse sufficient discontent to force a political settlement.

To what extent has Rhodesia been able to avoid sanctions through loopholes and leakages? How effective have these measures really been in denying Rhodesia access to foreign markets and foreign supplies? An important factor is that South Africa, Portugal, Mozambique, and South West Africa made no attempt to implement any sanctions—indeed, these states have been the major avenues of sanctions avoidance through trans-shipments of goods to and from Rhodesia. Zambia, although a major outlet for Rhodesian goods, particularly manufactures, was one of Rhodesia's greatest political foes. Nevertheless, "long-standing organic links between the two complementary economies"[20] could not be quickly dissolved without serious damage to Zambia. Although Zambia's imports declined sharply, its dependence upon Rhodesian products had been too great to allow a total embargo. Between 1965 and 1966 its imports decreased by roughly £36 million but still continued to exceed £20 million.[21] Zambia could not have reduced its dependence upon Rhodesian suppliers without major assistance from the great powers. Vital commodities, including petroleum, have been airlifted to Zambia in order to circumvent use of Rhodesian facilities. By mid-1967, Zambian imports had fallen to about 75 percent of earlier levels,[22] imposing severe constraints upon Zambia and demonstrating that sanctions can be more costly to the enforcing state than the target nation. Sales to Malawi, another neighboring political foe, while not as quantitatively important as to Zambia, have been in much the same position.

Other nations maintaining substantial trade with Rhodesia, despite official declarations to the contrary, are Japan, West Germany, Switzerland, and Belgium. The embargo's effectiveness was well summarized in a 1968 report:

> Voluntary sanctions by Britain and other countries reduced Rhodesian exports by 36 percent in the first year after UDI. In January 1967 there was a mandatory U.N. ban covering 60 percent of normal Rhodesian exports and 15 percent of normal imports. This barely reduced trade at all but expanded the loophole by which Rhodesian exports came into world markets clandestinely through South Africa or Mozambique middlemen. All OECD countries (except Portugal and Switzerland) have reduced direct trade with Rhodesia very substantially. . . . A comparison of the trade figures . . . suggests that 80–85 percent of Rhodesian trade is now done with South Africa or Mozambique or through middlemen in those countries. In June 1968 another U.N. mandatory resolution came into effect banning all trade with, investments in, and air communications with Rhodesia. But the South African loophole remains wide open.[23]

In the United States, shipments to Rhodesia are governed under the Export Control Act. This act proscribes direct sales and prohibits the reexport to Rhodesia of American products bought by foreign purchasers. Known violations of the act have been minimal, although some have occurred, such as the export to Rhodesia of a cotton gin by a South African firm that had imported it from the United States. That company subsequently lost its right to import American goods. More recently, a subsidiary of Reynolds Metals pleaded guilty in late 1973 to importing Rhodesian petalite illegally. There have been other violations involving American goods, but overall the number reported is not large.

Defensive Measure and Overall Trade Impact

Rhodesian exchange controls and import restrictions were implemented and stringently enforced after British sanctions were levied. In addition, rationing of some products—the most important was gasoline—was enacted. Under the quota system instituted, luxury imports are all but impossible. The system is so arranged that import volumes depend upon the foreign exchange situation, that is, the progress of exports. Four times annually the Treasury, in cooperation with the central bank, releases statistics on the amounts of foreign exchange available. The Ministry of Trade then allocates this sum among the demanders. Once the necessary foreign exchange is obtained, there are apparently no local restrictions upon the sources of supply chosen. Left to their own initiative, Rhodesian importers (and exporters) have been able to maintain external contacts by means of numerous clandestine and shifting actions. In short, sanctions have failed to produce sufficiently serious trade disruptions to bring Rhodesia's economy to a halt. One respondent in a 1969 survey taken by this writer volunteered the following:

> I have worked 63 years in export/import and have never seen a boycott which was really effective! F. i. [sic] *the present boycott of Rhodesia is a farce* [italics added].

Export sanctions have been largely avoided through trade of unmarked or fraudulently marked goods with South Africa and Mozambique.[24] Only Rhodesian tobacco has been significantly affected. Rhodesian tobacco is of high quality and rather distinctive, and its origin is easy to determine by experts. The ease of identification, coupled with the availability of numerous other world market suppliers, has caused significant decline in tobacco sales, once Rhodesia's leading export. In addition, the prices obtained have been far lower than would otherwise have been the case. Tobacco, it should be stressed, is still exported, but arrangements have been made under the cloak of great secrecy, using techniques ordinarily restricted to television spy programs! Exports of minerals, beef, cotton, and a number of items have been maintained and even increased during a decade of sanctions. Establishing dummy importing organizations in third countries and shuffling subsidiaries are frequent techniques utilized by businessmen (in the boycotting states) to avoid detection. Ironically, some Rhodesian products were still selling in Britain as late as 1969, brought in under a number of guises.

Import sanctions have been wholly ineffective. Rhodesia has purchased whenever it wanted to. Such purchases have occurred in almost every market of the world through third-party intermediaries. The effect of sanctions has been to curtail imports by reducing foreign exchange earnings rather than by exporters worldwide shunning trade with Rhodesia. Only the import of oil has led to major, but not insurmountable, difficulties.

Oil sanctions were introduced by Britain on December 17, 1965. The United States followed suit, as did other oil producers. Prime Minister Smith then introduced gasoline rationing and established a government purchasing company, Genta, to procure oil in the face of the embargo. It was originally thought, particularly in British circles (which consistently overestimated the potential impact of sanctions), that the oil boycott would soon bring Rhodesia to its knees. However, oil was needed for only 27 percent of Rhodesia's power, with 10 percent coming from the Kariba hydroelectric facilities and the remaining 63 percent coming from solid fuels mined at Wankie.[25] Nevertheless, the total cessation of oil imports would have been highly disruptive, witness U.S. disruptions when dependent upon a smaller percentage of energy supplied by embargoing Arab states. Despite oil sanctions, supplies from unknown dealers and transported on mysterious tankers began porting in Mozambique. From there the oil went by pipeline to a relatively new Rhodesian refinery that processed petroleum for both Zambia and Rhodesia. When the owners of the storage tanks in Beira disallowed use of their facilities, construction of storage tanks in Rhodesia was undertaken. The blatant violations of oil sanctions prompted the U.N. Security Council to authorize a British blockade of the Beira port to vessels with Rhodesia-bound oil.

Oil supplies then began entering from other sources. In the early years, most came by road from South Africa, being trucked over the Great North Road and entering Rhodesia at Beitbridge on the Limpopo River. By mid-February 1966 this route brought in at least 35,000 gallons a day, and by the third week in March this figure had more than doubled.[26] There are now other routes, generally unknown to the outside world, involving both rail and truck. Large storage tanks have been built in strategic locations, and petroleum has been stockpiled. In addition to domestic economizing, petroleum supplies to Zambia were discontinued. The oil embargo, then, caused problems but delivered no crushing economic blows. Interestingly, by early 1967 Zambia was experiencing such shortages that motorists were crossing into Rhodesia to fill their cars with gas.[27] As one economist has written,

> The oil embargo was never really a serious threat to the viability of the . . . economy. It had certain psychological effects—particularly the turning back of tankers in the Mozambique channel. It has created difficulties for the motor trade, for oil companies, for the pipeline company and also forced the closure of the oil refinery. The extra cost of importing fuel by road and rail has pushed up prices and production costs in the economy. However, the measure of the embargo's ineffectiveness is that petrol is rationed only through the price mechanism. A consumer can purchase as much fuel as he requires provided he is prepared to pay the surcharge. . . .[28]

Gasoline rationing was intermittently eased, then eliminated. More damaging was the Arab oil embargo, which reduced flows to South Africa and Portugal, who in turn reduced their supplies to Rhodesia. Gasoline rationing was reintroduced in February 1974.

Table 10 lists exports, imports, and the trade balances for 1965–75. The table clearly shows the substantial drop in exports—some 34.8 percent—from 1965 to 1966, a decline that can be considered the direct result of the sanctions. Export volumes, particularly influenced by the success of sanctions on tobacco, remained quite low until 1969, when a sharp upturn was registered. Since that time, annual increases have been steady and substantial, although it was not until 1972 that export values reattained (and surpassed) their presanctions level. Rising exports can be attributed to the healthy world market for products such as chrome ore, asbestos, and coal, a market in which world importers became progressively less "concerned" about the source of their purchases. Another cause of rising exports was the economy's internal adjustment to sanctions.

Imports fell sharply—by 25.4 percent—during 1966, reflecting domestic economizing and exchange control activities. Imports represented 37 percent of the gross domestic product in 1965, but this figure fell to 16.7 percent in 1966.[29] Imports increased steadily after 1966, mainly because of strong growth in the economy and availability of the necessary foreign exchange. Nevertheless, they did not reach 1965 levels until early 1971. Deficits existed in only

TABLE 10
Exports, Imports and Trade Balance of Rhodesia, 1965–75
(includes gold and reexports)
R$

Year	Exports	Imports	Balance
1965	323.0	245.9	77.1
1966	210.4	183.4	27.0
1967	212.2	199.9	12.3
1968	193.9	219.9	−26.0
1969	231.8	204.1	27.7
1970	265.3	242.2	23.1
1971	290.1	291.7	−1.6
1972	345.3	287.1	58.2
1973	N.A.	N.A.	83.0
1974	N.A.	N.A.	50.8
1975	N.A.	N.A.	33.1

Sources: *Economic Survey of Rhodesia,* annuals for 1965, 1966, 1969, 1970, 1971, 1972, 1973, and 1975 (Salisbury: Government Printer).

two of the eleven years covered. For 1971 the deficit was negligible (R$ 1.6 million). The sizable deficit (R$ 26 million) of 1968 was mainly the result of a severe drought-induced disaster in agriculture, although a partial explanation lies in the tightening of sanctions occurring that year. While favorable trade balances have been the rule, with the exception of 1973 the substantial presanctions positive balance of R$ 77.1 million (1965) has not been approximated.

The reduced size of the favorable trade accounts has harmed the current account position. Diminished net trade revenues coupled with invisibles shortfalls have resulted in current account deficits in eight of ten years (see Table 11). Rhodesia has traditionally had deficits in the invisibles accounts. After UDI the invisibles deficit (R$ 51 million in 1965) fell as the volume of trade was reduced, hitting a low of R$ 24.1 million in 1968. Since that year there has been a steady rise, at an increasing rate, in the size of this shortfall. The 1973 deficit jumped to R$ 100.5 million, with even larger deficits in 1974 (R$ 146.4 million) and 1975 (R$ 161.1 million). These substantial increases are clearly related to sanctions. The need to route so much foreign trade through South Africa has increased transportation costs. Port congestion in South Africa was severe for most of the first half of the 1970s. There have been serious delays in loading and unloading, and an increase in port fees and related expenses. A major cause of the almost doubling of

TABLE 11

Balance of Payments: Current and Capital Transactions, 1966–75

(R$ million)

	1966	1967	1968	1969	1970	1971	1972	1973	1974	1975	1966–75
Merchandise, net[a]	27.0	12.3	−26.0	27.7	23.1	−1.6	58.2	83.0	50.8	33.1	287.6
Invisible transactions, net	−31.3	−29.0	−24.1	−24.2	−37.1	−55.8	−57.4	−100.5	−146.4	−161.1	−666.9
Capital transactions, net	−4.6	23.7	39.5	9.9	26.3	30.5	−2.3	51.6	62.6	101.9	338.5
Short-term financing, changes in banking reserves, errors and omissions	−8.9	7.0	−10.6	13.4	12.3	−26.9	−1.6	34.2	−33.1	−26.6	−40.8

[a] Allowance has been made for nonmonetary gold, internal freight to border, timing and coverage adjustments in the computation of merchandise trade.

Source: Ministry of Finance, *Economic Survey of Rhodesia, 1975*, Salisbury.

the invisibles deficit (and tripling of the deficit in services) in 1973 was the closing of the Zambia border, which cost Rhodesia earnings on transit freight to and from Zambia. In 1975 the new regime in independent Mozambique closed its border, again denying Rhodesia transit earnings as well as closing its ports to Rhodesian trade. Finally, there has been a steady rise in outflows because of dividend and interest payments to investors outside Rhodesia.

With the size of the favorable trade balance declining and the invisibles deficits soaring, capital inflows have been necessary to maintain import levels without undue loss of reserves. The decade under sanctions has been characterized by substantial overseas investment, mostly from South Africa. Inflows over the 1966–75 period totaled almost R$ 340 million. In the post-UDI years through 1973, capital inflows were sufficient to yield an overall balance of payments surplus of R$19 million. Despite continued growth in foreign investment, 1974 and 1975 witnessed overall deficits due to significant current account shortfalls. The world recession in 1974–75 was without doubt the major cause of the weakened trade balance. The diversion of resources to national defense constitutes another cause. Balance-of-payments problems in 1976 and 1977 have been reflected in reduced foreign exchange allocations. Without question, the stepping up of terrorist activities and the continued political uncertainties have been major negative influences limiting expansion of capital inflows. Nevertheless, the import of long-term capital has enabled Rhodesia to maintain imports in the face of the substantial current accounts deficits.[30]

To maintain its export markets, Rhodesia has had to sell its products at prices lower than normal.[31] At the same time, to retain suppliers Rhodesia has been forced to pay higher prices. Costs have been pushed up by a risk-premium and by greater transport and middlemen expenses resulting from South African port congestion and circuitous trade routings to avoid detection. On the other hand, before the onset of the world economic slowdown Rhodesia was assisted in its export prices by a buoyant demand for several of its products. Official Rhodesian statistics show annual changes in the terms of trade fluctuating up-and-down. The terms of trade deteriorated some 18 percent from 1965 to 1966, mainly as a result of sanctions. The index has fluctuated but on net balance improved only marginally, from 82.3 in 1966 to 85.1 in 1973.[32] While the deterioration over the 1965–66 period is clearly the result of sanctions, it is not possible to ascertain what part, if any, of the annual changes in the terms of trade index since that time is the result of, or related to, sanctions.

Sanctions have clearly had an impact upon Rhodesia's external accounts, but the economy remains an export-oriented one. Describing economic prospects for the post–1975 recession years, official Rhodesian sources have written that "any significant recovery in Rhodesia must be export-led."[33] The progress of exports seems to be more affected by the health of the world economy than by sanctions. Manufacturing, mining, and agriculture currently each account for roughly one-third of export revenues.

The border with Mozambique was officially closed by the new, independent government in late June 1975, amid resolute statements by African leaders predicting the Rhodesian regime's downfall as a result of being sealed off so substantially. Here again it is of interest to note the costs of sanctions enforcement to the enforcing state. Mozambique has lost revenues by denying use of its ports. Indeed, at the British Commonwealth Conference in May 1975, Mozambique was promised compensation for these foregone fees. Further, a completely closed border means that transit traffic across Rhodesia between the coast and several black African states must terminate, thus denying the least expensive transport routes to these nations. Neil McInnes's prognostications are of interest in this regard:

> If the Africans, at British instigation, were literally to shut their borders with Rhodesia, they would face starvation. Salisbury can rely on that circumstance to ensure that the public blockade is tempered by many surreptitious exceptions. . . . Rhodesia and South Africa have become the breadbasket of sub-Saharan Africa. . . . the only countries in the region to have increased their per capita agricultural output since 1960. . . . The Rhodesians consume 3.5 million tons of corn and export 11 million tons to their neighbors. . . . Kenya's corn yields are one-quarter of Rhodesia's. . . Zambia, Mozambique—and above all Tanzania—face grave agricultural problems. . . .[34]

These sentiments have been underscored by a number of sources reporting that Organization of African Unity officials have received bribes to ignore sanctions violations. It appears clear that clandestine trade is occurring.

Relations with South Africa—commercial and political—remain strong but show evidence of strain. South Africa has been actively seeking a rapprochement with the black African states, who in turn insist that South Africa reduce its support for Rhodesia. South Africa removed its police (which helped patrol the border) from Rhodesia and has applied pressure upon Ian Smith to reach agreement with local African leaders. Rhodesia's ability to withstand sanctions would be greatly reduced if South Africa no longer cooperated.

Impact Upon the Domestic Economy

The British renunciation of the use of armed force dictates that policy change must come from within Rhodesia, but it is to be induced through external economic pressures—trade and financial sanctions. These pressures, if successful, are to result in falling real incomes, increasing unemployment, inflation, and a variety of other domestically undersirable outcomes that would either prompt substantial emigration of white Rhodesians, thus seriously reducing the viability of the present socioeconomic structure, or create economic dislocations sufficient to make the populace reconsider the politics of the Smith regime. In short, meaningful domestic economic declines are absolutely necessary to bring about sufficient demands upon the government to change its policies.

British financial sanctions did create several dislocations and have reduced Rhodesia's long-term ability to import, both by freezing London-held reserves and by excluding Rhodesia from the sterling area. Rhodesia was forced to demand payment for its exports in nonsterling hard currencies, and this, no doubt, has reduced total export earnings. Ironically, however, Rhodesian countermeasures reversed the intended damages in the short-run. Despite the freeze on its London reserves, Rhodesia claimed to hold £12 million outside London (although this figure may have been "puffed" for the purpose of assuring suppliers of adequate means of payment). Just prior to UDI, Rhodesia's total reserves were approximately £28 million, and on December 16, 1966, the last date of quoted figures, reserves stood at £21.6 million. In response to United Kingdom financial measures, Rhodesia repudiated its debt obligations in London and to the World Bank, which were estimated at £108 million.[35] The blocking of payments inflows to Rhodesia by both Britain and Zambia amounted to "£5.1 million 1966 while Rhodesia's retaliatory measures reduced the income paid abroad by £8.8 million—leaving a net gain of £3.7 million."[36] The net result of the financial sanctions and countersanctions seems to have placed Rhodesia in a superior rather than inferior position for the first several years of sanctions.

Traditionally, Rhodesian banks relied upon London money markets. Financial sanctions limited them to domestic resources for securing and investing funds.

> The isolation of the Rhodesian banking system however took place at a moment of strong liquidity because . . . of the halt put to transfers for service, dividend and capital payments to Commonwealth countries . . . which normally would have found their way to London.[37]

Liquidity was further strengthened by import restrictions. Accordingly, there was an extraordinary volume of liquidity that suggests strong inflationary pressures. Treasury and central bank control policies helped curb inflation. As early as November 1965, the month of UDI, government loans totaling £20 million were issued and fully suscribed, drawing backing from investors who would previously have channeled the funds abroad. A national saving campaign directed toward the "man in the street" was implemented. The central bank manipulated reserve requirements and in additon issued a number of moral suasion directives. Despite these measures strong inflationary pressures, emanating from a variety of sources, remained.

As indicated, tobacco has been very important in the Rhodesian economy. It is purchased from the farmers at fixed and graded prices by the Tobacco Corporation, whose task it is to dispose of the crop. The effectiveness of sanctions has resulted in significant governmental crop restriction efforts. Table 12 is a summary of the tobacco industry from 1965–69. The prosperity of 1965 had led to an increased tobacco harvest in 1966. However, the difficulties encountered in exporting led to a sharp contraction in the planned crop for 1967. Table 12 clearly shows the very significant contraction in the size of the annual harvests, with the 1968 crop

TABLE 12
Rhodesian Tobacco Industry, 1965–69

Year	Crop Weight[a]	Announced Av. Price (pence per pound)	Expected Income[b] for Growers (£ millions)
1965	111.6	32.96	33.8
1966	117.9	24.00	26.0
1967	90.7	28.00	23.3
1968	59.9	28.00	15.4
1969	62.3	25.00	13.7

[a]thousands of metric tons

[b]Actual incomes earned were probably lower due to particularly harsh grading by the Tobacco Corporation, which then made purchases at rates even lower than the announced ones.

Sources: Hawkins, "The Rhodesian Economy under Sanctions," p. 55; Economist Intelligence Unit, *Rhodesia, Zambia, Malawi: Quarterly Economic Review* 2(1969), p. 8.

being only 50 percent of the 1966 figure. The 1970 and 1971 crops remained at the 1969 level, with 1972 witnessing an allowed increase to 66,000 metric tons. In addition, the average announced purchase prices have been far below the 1965 level. The result has been that tobacco growers' income fell by about 75 percent during the first several years of sanctions.

Before UDI there were about 3,600 tobacco growers; by May 1975 only 1600 remained.[38] The government actively encouraged agricultural diversifications, so this large exodus was anticipated. Nevertheless, it has led to a decline in total agricultural employment because tobacco is a more labor-intensive crop than the most promising substitutes, maize and cotton. Further, industries within the economy dependent upon buoyant tobacco conditions have also been harmed. While increases in the production of other crops have tended to counter this decline, these expansions elsewhere in agriculture did not fully offset tobacco employment cutbacks until 1970. On the positive side, crop reductions tended to ease the balance of payments situation, since roughly one-fifth of the industry's inputs have been imported.

The Tobacco Corporation has had great difficulty in disposing of the crop, despite severe price reductions as inducements to purchase. Probably only 120 million pounds of the 1966 crop—less than half—were sold that year.[39] The stockpile in the early months of 1969 was roughly 300 million pounds.[40] Precipitously sharp dislocations in the industry were avoided through the Tobacco Corporation's purchasing, even though exports have been seriously curtailed. Toward the end of 1968 it was announced that the "total cost of stockpiling excess tobacco from the 1966 and 1967 crops, together with losses on sales already affected, amounted to more than £32 million. . . ."[41] Production quotas ended at the beginning of the 1973–74 season, the post-UDI stockpile having been sold. Tobacco reverted to open auction in March 1974. Strong prices led to the withdrawal of government price supports. Prices in the spring of 1975, however, were appallingly low because of increased production, lessened demand by international manufacturers who drew on stockpiles, and uncertainly over the ability to export from Momzabique. Tobacco's long-run outlook is poor as long as sanctions remain. Grower discontent remains considerable. The farmers, however, are relatively few in number and the regime, although taking great pains to ease transitional problems, has in general been able to ignore most of their protests. Further, the farmers are among the most staunch backers of UDI. Despite their economic vulnerabilty to sanctions, they are unlikely to pressure Smith toward an accommodation with Great Britain.

Raw sugar had become an important export for Rhodesia by the early 1960s, and the industry began to grow rapidly; however, the exceptional instabilities in world sugar prices coupled with slumping prices dealt a severe blow to this industry even before sanctions were implemented. Thus, in 1964 Rhodesia exported about 96,000 tons of raw sugar and earned almost $10 million. The following year exports nearly tripled, but prices had fallen so much that earnings were $7,000 less than the previous year.[42] To ease sales declines in the face of sanctions and slumping prices in the late 1960s, the government stockpiled sugar. It also encouraged planting cotton, wheat, peanuts, cereals, and raising cattle.

Cotton production, stimulated by guaranteed government prices, has increased significantly. Approximately one-third of the cotton is consumed within Rhodesia and another third exported to South Africa. The remainder must be sold on world markets. Corn output has also greatly increased. Rhodesia's principal crops in the early 1970s (in terms of physical volume) ranked as follows: sugar, corn, millet, peanuts, cottonseed, tobacco, sorghum, and cotton.[43] However, this agricultural diversification and import substitution has neither been easy nor costless, and this is especially true with respect to the substitutes for tobacco. With the exception of cotton, productivity was higher in tobacco pursuits than in substitute areas. For example, before sanctions a given set of inputs devoted to tobacco may have earned $100 in foreign exchange, with those earnings in turn commanding 100 bushels of corn. The same resources are now directly producing corn within Rhodesia, but only yield 80 bushels. Although these numbers are merely illustrative, the effect is quite real. This forced import substitution is yet another source of inflationary pressure.

Essentially due to the tobacco cutbacks, agriculture's contribution to the gross domestic product fell from £69.1 million in 1965 to £67.8 million (1966). Over the 1955–65 period, agriculture (European and African) accounted for roughly 20 percent of the gross domestic product. This figure fell to 15.9 percent in the drought year 1968 and appears to have stabilized in the 16–17 percent range for the first portion of the 1970s.[44] Most of this decline is in European agriculture, with its contribution to the GDP falling from 12.9 percent in 1965 to 8.9 percent in 1968.[45] Despite the dislocations wrought by sanctions, there has nonetheless been a remarkable expansion in the volume of output, which rose by more than 80 percent over the 1964–74 period.[46] African agriculture has not fared so well, although in terms of an historical development process some think it has been positively affected by sanctions by stimulation of a larger cash-crop sector.

> In 1965, for instance, out of a gross output worth $34.7 million, almost 80 percent represented subsistence production. . . . By 1972, this ratio had fallen 69 percent, because the cash production of black farmers had trebled from $8.3 million in 1965 to $24.9 million in 1972. This is partly a reflection of the growth in the importance of cotton. . . .[47]

In other sectors of the economy, the sharpest declines registered over the 1966–67 period were in transport and communications. Sanctions were particulary damaging to the automobile industry as auto imports slowed and gasoline rationing was introduced. Shortly after UDI the large Ford and BMC motor assembly plants, which were foreign owned, ceased production. They were reopened in December 1965, under Rhodesian control, but forced to close again for a period in 1967 because of a lack of imported spare parts. The reopenings created roughly 1,000 additional jobs, but both plants, cut off from their parent companies, have been operating below capacity. The chemical and petroleum products field was also considerably depressed for several years.

Minerals have generally been the products most easily exported since the imposition of sanctions. While the actual volume of mining output fell marginally in 1966, the "value of mining output rose 2 percent above its 1965 level."[48] In 1965 asbestos was the most important mineral for sales abroad, followed by gold, copper, chrome, and coal. Iron ore output has been expanding, both to meet increasing local needs for steel and for export, particularly to Japan. Further, in 1968, the Anglo-American Corporation of South Africa began construction on a new nickel enterprise. Rising world prices for these minerals in the late 1960s and early 1970s encouraged production. Mining and quarrying produced a 1968 output of R$ 84.7 million, the figures rising to R$ 105.7 in 1969 and reaching R$ 122.8 million in 1970.[49] The value of industry output increased by more than 200 percent from 1965 to 1973. Hence, although a prime target of sanctions, the mining sector on the whole prospers and is an important source of export revenues.

Turning to the manufacturing sector, the expansion of markets under the Federation proved a major impetus to growth. Despite dissolution, the Zambian market in particular remained a significant outlet for manufactured goods. After UDI, Zambian imports began to decline steadily. The relatively large market had allowed certain economies of scale and in spite of a redirection of manufactured exports to South Africa (some of which no doubt ended up in Zambia again), the export market shrinkage probably resulted in cost increases. The index of manufacturing production (using 1964 as a base) had risen to 108 in 1965 and then fell to 101 in 1966 as sanctions were felt. With the exception of foodstuffs and electricity, each major area of manufacturing activity in 1966 was below its 1965 levels. In 1967, however, the index returned to its 1965 level.[50] Beverages and tobacco had recovered to just about 1965 levels, while metals and metal products, which had only slightly dipped, rose to an index of 113, five points above the 1965 level. The greatest advances were made in textiles and clothing output, which soared to 120 from a 1966 index of 103. Only tobacco grading and packing continued to decline. The 1967 index for these activities was 64, again reflecting how deeply sanctions have cut into this field.[51]

Emphasis has been on industrial diversification and import substitution. The textiles industry is a good case in point. Agricultural diversification has resulted in increasing cotton outputs, and this raw material has been used for supplying a growing textile industry that has been producing import substitutes. Further, import controls stimulated demand for a wide range of locally produced goods and the production response, both for home consumption and for a limited amount of export, has been quite good. Interestingly, some 250 new factories were established between UDI and August 1967.[52] Indeed, Rhodesian manufacturers have pursued the South African market (as the Zambian one grew smaller) with such vigor that South African businessmen began demanding protection from Rhodesian products. This particularly irked the Rhodesians since South Africa has replaced much of the lost Zambian market. Under South African pressure the Smith regime was forced in 1968 to place "voluntary" restraints upon exports of textiles, shoes, and radios to South Africa. In short, manufacturing industries on the whole have not suffered greatly because of sanctions, although costs have certainly risen. The Rhodesian public has proved amenable to many new brand names and numerous previously imported items are now domestically produced. The quality of these items was at first poor but has improved.

Sanctions may be viewed as a form of involuntary protection and, if infant industry potential exists, are likely to foster the growth of economically efficient production—production which might not otherwise have been given the opportunity to develop or display its potential. Manufacturing activities in the 1960–65 period accounted for roughly 16–18 percent of GDP. By 1970 the figure reached 22.2 percent and in 1972 stood at 23.2 percent, larger than mining and agriculture combined.[53] Ironically, then, it is possible that sanctions may yield some important benefits to Rhodesia if infant industry potential does exist. It is as yet somewhat difficult to judge, particularly because the guerrilla war and the political uncertainties have muddled the picture so much it is difficult to assess effects. These empirical findings conform to the conclusions of the Curtin and Murray study of 1967, which suggested that Rhodesian industry was rather sophisticated and, therefore, well placed to withstand the impact of sanctions. Their findings indicated that the scope for successful import substitution was large, provided that certain vital imports could be obtained. In sum, Rhodesian manufacturing on the whole felt only marginal damage and under the umbrella of sanctions has expanded and prospered.

It is interesting and logical that the building and construction fields enjoyed an upsurge after sanctions were imposed. With foreign investment limited by exchange controls, while the propensity to save was stimulated both by government efforts and some general apprehension about the future, investment in private housing boomed as funds denied other outlets were channeled into construction. In addition, increased spending by the government, particularly on African housing projects, also stimulated this industry. As construction picked up, some of the negative employment and income effects of sanctions in other areas were offset.

The structure of post-UDI industrial development is somewhat indicated by a comparison of total industrial production, whose index reached 198.3 (1964 = 100) in 1975, to the various specific industry groups. Those falling substantially below the overall index were drink and tobacco (159.4), transport equipment and workshops (104.2), and clothing and footwear (149.6), a field initially stimulated by sanctions. Those areas substantially ahead include textiles (282.3), metals and metal products (294.3), and nonmetallic mineral products (276.2).[55] The index for all manufacturing groups stood at 204.3, six points above the index for all industrial production. It is noteworthy that Rhodesia's rate of growth in industrial production tripled the corresponding figure for the United States.

Sanctions have altered both the sectoral origins of national output and the distribution of income as well. Trade theory posits that participation in international trade makes a nation's scarce factors less scarce; trade barriers, on the other hand, made them scarcer. Relatively abundant factors become more valuable through participation in trade, and less so if a nation withdraws from trade. Because Rhodesia's economic system is basically market-directed, with prices responding to supply and demand, rates of return to the various factors tend to reflect these underlying valuations. The relatively scarce factors in Rhodesia are capital and skilled labor, including managerial and entrepreneurial skills. Unskilled labor, though, is the relatively abundant factor.

Any withdrawal from trade would tend to increase relative rates of return to owners of capital and skilled labor and reduce returns to unskilled labor.

An understanding of the possible effects of sanctions upon the distribution of income may be made easier by viewing the presanctions economy as divided into three sectors: export industries; import competitive industries; and the nontrade sector (for example, sevices such as haircuts). With the imposition of sanctions, returns to all factors in the export sector will tend to fall. Returns to all factors in the import competitive industries will rise absolutely. Real returns will later be reduced as resources leaving the export sector enter import substitution. Both the degree of rise and subsequent retrenchment will depend upon the elasticities of factor demand and supply and the input mixes. In the nontrade sector, initially the returns to the scarce factors will rise (because of the withdrawal from trade, which makes them even scarcer), but real returns will later be diminished by the entry of resources from the shrinking export industries. Again, the degree of rise and subsequent reduction will depend upon factor demand and supply elasticities and the relevant production functions. For the abundant factor—unskilled labor—real returns will tend to fall due to inflows of labor released from the export sector. In short, both participation in trade and withdrawal from it will alter the domestic distribution of income. With a reduction in the export sector, it is certain that the *absolute real return to unskilled labor in the nontrade sector will fall,* while the return to the scarce factors will be subject to opposing influences. *In the import competitive fields returns to both factors will be subject to opposing pressures.*

Withdrawal from trade will reduce the real national dividend as well as alter its distribution. It is possible, however, that despite the reduction in real output, the relative share of owners of the scarce factors may so increase that their real income as a group rises. If this were the case, not only would the full weight of sanctions fall upon the owners of the abundant factors (Africans), but such owners would bear an even greater burden. That is, it is conceivable for sanctions to reduce the real national income by, say X dollars, but reduce the absolute level of living of Africans by $X + Y$ dollars (while at the same time raising the absolute level of living of whites!)

Because the abundant factor, unskilled labor, is forced out of its most profitable use in the export sector, it must either (1) accept lower returns elsewhere, or, if unable to find alternative wage employment, (2) accept unemployment or withdraw from the money economy and return to the subsistence sector. Given the minimum wage and "rate for the job" (akin to equal pay for equal work) legislation, low marginal productivity is likely to make it uneconomical to hire unskilled laborers in sufficiently large numbers, thus thrusting them into unemployment or withdrawal from the money economy. Table 6 presented the distribution of employment in 1965. Tobacco, formerly the leading export and a relatively labor-intensive industry, suffered a significant decline. As the table indicates, for non-Africans this sector was not a major provider of jobs. For Africans, on the other hand, it was by far *the major* employment sector. Overall, employment of Africans fell some 9,000 in 1966 alone,[56] and continued to decline in 1967. Although sanctions did result in some white unemployment, it was minimal and generally only temporary. The adjustment to sanctions brought about a changed pattern of employment. The distribution sector, weakened by the decline in external trade and an increased average propensity to save, was adversely affected, with both white and black employment down by over 8 percent. The increase in government activities, on the other hand, resulted in an increase (8.1 percent) for whites in its employ, with the number of Africans also increasing somewhat. Last, the expanding building trades increased their employment, particularly of Africans (up 5.1 percent).[57] In terms of total employment, non-Africans did not experience declines. The Smith regime has been careful to maintain white employment. The picture is different for nonwhites. "No estimates are available on the number of Africans rendered jobless as a direct result of sanctions, though the emigration of over 21,000 male Africans in 1966 and 1967 gives a pointer."[58] Before UDI, rising African unemployment had been a problem and sanctions only exacerbated it. To mitigate increasing African unemployment, the government instituted manpower controls in several industries. In addition, steps were taken to prohibit the employment of nonlocal Africans.

In short, *in terms of employment the brunt of sanctions has fallen upon the Africans*, obviously not the intention of the boycott initiators and not a group that can place serious political pressure upon the regime. By 1968, however, employment of both whites and nonwhites increased, the year marking a reversal in the declining trend in African employment.[59] In 1966 there were 644,000 employed Africans. By 1970, 788,000 were employed and in 1975 there were 945,000 Africans with jobs in the money economy.[60]

Perhaps the best barometer of Rhodesia's economic health under sanctions is the annual rate of real growth. The gross domestic product (1964 prices), which had risen in 1965, fell by 5.06 percent in 1966.[61] This decline may be considered the direct result of sanctions. When adjusted for population increase, the per capita decline was even greater, although this factor had little effect upon the white electorate since the bulk of population growth was African. From 1967 through 1974, however, the real annual growth rate averaged almost 8 percent,[62] a creditable record by international standards and one particularly satisfying when compared to the economic stagnation of the first half of the 1960s. Recovery had clearly been in evidence by 1965 but was delayed by the imposition of sanctions. In the absence of the embargo the economy undoubtedly would have expanded even faster, though along somewhat different paths; however, only in 1966 was growth stifled. "Investment as a ratio of GDP fell in 1966 to 12.3 percent—its lowest level on record."[63] With relatively low interest rates and returned business confidence, however, investment greatly strengthened (reaching 21.9 percent of GDP in 1973), thus playing an important role in the continued economic advance. The world recession had a significant impact upon Rhodesia, and 1975 witnessed the first economic downturn since 1966. Two additional factors contributing to the depth of Rhodesia's recession were the decline in business confidence because of increasing terrorism and the increased proportion of resources being allocated to military activities. To summarize, sanctions have clearly failed to extinguish economic growth. To the contrary, Rhodesia has enjoyed significant prosperity.

The domestic discontent that was to have been stirred by the dislocations caused by sanctions occurred only on a limited basis, and mainly in one year. Further, "the share of wages and salaries in national income actually increased in 1966 due to the sharp fall in profits."[64] White employees, the most important group within the electorate, emerged virtually unscathed from sanctions. In fact, in that year there was a rise "in average white earnings . . . of 3.4

percent which was the result of redistribution away from profits and African employees earnings."[65] Interestingly, the share of profits climbed steeply in 1967 and 1968, in part reflecting the growth of a new class of small manufacturers who emerged to supply import substitutes. The only group in the electorate to suffer serious harm were tobacco farmers who, despite economic vulnerability, were among the staunchest supporters of UDI. Their pressures upon the regime have not been in favor of accommodation but rather for increased subsidies for themselves. In short, the white community's standard of living was protected even in the face of absolute declines, and this was a major reason sanctions have failed to induce the political change the boycotting states desired. The earlier mentioned possibility, however, of real white levels of living increasing in the face of a falling national output (1966) does not appear to have prevailed. Sanctions may be deemed a failure if their prime goal was to bring about renunciation of UDI through external economic pressures because aggregate output rose on a substantial basis since 1967.

The African population has borne most of the impact of sanctions. African employment was heavily concentrated in tobacco, and the success of sanctions in this area caused much unemployment and rural dislocations. The Duncan study found that real African farm incomes dropped 16 percent over 1963–71, with the African farm worker's wage "less than half the average received by his counterpart in mining, and about a quarter of that received by Africans in the manufacturing industry."[66] Nor has African unemployment been restricted to sectors directly touched by sanctions. Sutcliff reports that in the urban sector and in civil service some relatively high-earning blacks have been released in order to provide jobs for whites displaced by sanctions.[67] Given the 3.5 percent annual increase in the African population, it is obvious that real per capita incomes were seriously eroded in 1966. The absolute wage gap between whites and Africans grew by about 40 percent over 1965–72.[68] Sanctions also disrupted the traditional development process by forcing displaced African urbanites to return to the subsistence sector. This interruption, however, was countered by a longer term impact mentioned earlier, namely, the increase in the size of the cash-crop sector caused by sanctions induced agricultural restructuring.

There have been a variety of inflationary pressures related to sanctions. These include (1) the reduction in the supply of foreign goods; (2) the initial reduction in domestic output because of production disruptions caused by a lack of raw materials, spare parts, and other sanctions-related problems; (3) the higher price of most imports; (4) government spending for job creation and the stockpiling of tobacco; and (5) the high degree of liquidity in the economy with the halting of dividend, interest, and capital repayments that would have gone to London. Nevertheless, consumer price indices evidenced only moderate increases. Using 1964 as the base, the 1970 index of European consumer prices was only 115.6; for 1975 it was 149.2. For Africans, the 1970 index was 112.4, reaching 144.0 in 1975.[69] For the period 1965–75, the overall European price index rose 47.5 points. This compares quite favorably with inflation rates in Britain or the United States, where the price index for that same period rose 66.7 points.

The pattern of inflation gives some insight concerning the impact of sanctions. European transport prices rose more rapidly than did the general European index. Cloth and footwear, on the other hand, reflecting successful import substitution, had indices below average. The European foodstuffs index ran higher than the overall European price index through 1968, mirroring the higher costs of import substitutes. From 1969–73, however, the overall index and the foodstuffs figure were more or less equal, suggesting that experience with new crops had begun to yield productivity gains. Interestingly, the only factor accounting for the larger overall rise in the European price index than the African index is servants' wages. This category, which is not calculated in the African index, rose almost 55 percent over the 1965–75 period. Last, no discussion of Rhodesian price increases is complete without some mention of product quality, which clearly declined in the early years under sanctions and in many areas is still not commensurate with former imports. This aspect of inflation is real and visible but is not reflected in the price indices. Given the multitude of inflationary pressures, the relatively low rates of inflation merit explanation.

The government has skillfully blended monetary and fiscal policy to battle price level pressures. A national saving program directed at "the man in the street" was immediately implemented. Many investors who otherwise would have channeled funds abroad invested in government bonds. Bond issues have been repeatedly

floated and continually oversubscribed. In addition, public finance
has been dominated by a generally "orthodox" economic
philosophy that eschews deficits unless absolutely necessary. This
explains the reduced purchase prices and crop goals for tobacco,
implemented despite political unpopularity. Additionally, since
UDI a price control mechanism, freezing profit margins for a
specified list of items and limiting increases on others, has been in
effect. The controls have been flexible, thus allowing market
pressures to make themselves felt. Further, much of their success
derives from the fiscal restraint exercised, so that serious price
distortions have not resulted. Finally, the central bank has
manipulated reserve requirements and issued moral suasion
directives that have cooled inflationary pressures.

The 1969 tax reform brought some significant changes, reducing
income taxes, abolishing undistributed corporate profits taxes,
ending the surtax, and increasing sales taxations. Such measures
encourage saving and investment, important elements in
minimizing inflation. Another encouragement to investment has
been the generally low level of interest rates prevailing until recent
years. Because exchange control prevented the outflow of savings
in search of higher returns elsewhere, there was a remarkable
accumulation of funds. Demand tended to be easily satisfied at low
interest rates, and low inflation rates obviated any need to charge
an inflation premium. The ten-year average inflation rate prior to
1974 was below 3 percent, both for Europeans and Africans. Rising
oil prices and the world-wide inflation, however, brought Rhodesia
an inflation of over 7 percent in 1974 and 1975.

Two final domestic economic effects of sanctions merit comment.
The first is the reduced degree of competition within the economy. This has resulted principally from reduction in foreign
competition. Further, exchange control systems inevitably bear
most heavily upon new and smaller firms, which again tends to
lessen competition. Shrinkage in the volume of imports has also
reduced the minimal price/quality standards against which domestic
products would have been compared. A second and related impact
of sanctions is the growing degree of state interference. Price and
exchange controls, government marketing boards, statutory
bodies, state monopolies, and similar interventions have changed
the shape and operation of the Rhodesian economy. Past successful
economic performance appears to derive in large measure from the

vigor and dynamics of a market-directed system, but now it is possible that the numerous controls and interferences related to sanctions will reduce the productivity of the system and sap it of its dynamic elements. The Rhodesian businessman has, since UDI, persistently complained about growing state controls and their negative impacts, and the question of how far such controls can go without seriously impairing the efficiency of the economic structure is a continuing problem.

Sanctions also have noneconomic repercussions. Even before UDI the Smith regime had invoked a state of emergency because of the impending political crisis. After UDI, emergency powers were utilized frequently, and governmental controls over individual civil and political rights were exercised. Before sanctions a fluid political situation existed with opposition groups vocal in their opinions and their campaigning. In the face of sanctions, however, the regime has been able to stifle effectively opposition through censorship of the media, arrest and seizure of citizens or literature declared to be subversive and, hence, contrary to the interests and security of the country, and many other measures justified because the nation is under seige. In the fall of 1974, for example, the Roman Catholic Church weekly *Moto*, a publication frequently critical of the Smith government, was banned for having published "subversive" statements creating "hatred" between Africans and Europeans. It is interesting that this censorship and the arrests of political opposition have evoked only mild response from a white population generally accustomed to the full exercise of civil liberties; however, this accords with a frequent observation that censorship of ideas generally contrary to one's own is not likely to evoke much protest. The British undoubtedly had hoped that the more liberal political elements within Rhodesia and those groups most loyal to the Crown would be joined by Rhodesians undergoing economic hardships, so that the Smith regime would either be brought down or forced to change its policies. But the opposite result has prevailed. Effective political opposition has not been created but stifled, such repression ironically being justified by the necessity to face the economic warfare being waged by Britain and the United Nations.

A second impact relates to race relations. Prior to UDI there were few racial disturbances in Rhodesia, a minimum of *de jure* discrimination, and only a few similarities with South Africa's apartheid system. Sanctions, however, have reduced the influence of Rhodesian society's more liberal sphere and augmented the powers of the more racially conscious whites. Unquestionably, the degree of racial justice in Rhodesia has deteriorated since UDI. This deterioration, according to one knowledgeable observer, Professor W. H. Hutt, "is entirely due to circumstances created by sanctions." He continues:

> In my judgment Rhodesia *could* have given the world a copy-book example of how economic, social and political change of a revolutionary kind could occur without violence in a racially complex society.[70]

The racial progress and democracy of the pre-UDI days have been reversed and the apartheid system and its *de jure* discrimination is becoming institutionalized.

A third by-product of sanctions and their failure to produce capitulation is the growing terrorism and guerrilla warfare with which Rhodesia has had to cope. Without question, growth in African unemployment, repatriation of nonlocal Africans to surrounding areas, and frustrations of Africans at the failure of sanctions to deliver what they had expected have contributed to the very substantial rise in terrorism and armed conflict. Indeed, it is likely that change within Rhodesia, if it occurs, will be brought about by resort to violence and destruction, not by nonmilitary coercive activities such as sanctions. The regime has been forced to devote increasingly large amounts of resources to defense. In December 1972 the national service training period was extended from nine to twelve months, personnel exemptions for medical reasons were reduced, and increased efforts at nullifying "draft-dodging" were undertaken. A large number of additional measures were undertaken in 1974. In addition, terrorist activities have also played a role in reducing Rhodesia's tourist revenues.

Finally, sanctions could be deemed successful if their negative economic impacts were sufficiently strong to reduce levels of living to the point where immigration ceased and emigration soared. For the 1965–75 period, however, only in 1966 was there a net loss of Europeans.[71] That was the first full year of sanctions and 8,510 persons emigrated, apparently because of uncertainties caused by the embargo's imposition. Emigration continuously declined through 1972. Population inflows in 1966 were only 6,420, rising to

9,620 in 1967 and remaining above 10,900 in each of the next five years. Most immigrants are from South Africa, where the average wage earned by whites since 1965 continues to be below the corresponding Rhodesian figure. The number of immigrants in 1975 (12,430) attests to the continued attractiveness of Rhodesian levels of living. The Smith regime has undertaken extensive efforts to encourage immigration (including a five-year military exemption for newly arrived males) and discourage emigration. Because economic growth has been substantial, the increases in emigration since 1974 appear to reflect growing terrorist activities and increased military obligations imposed on the veteran population.[72] The first net loss of whites since 1966, some 7,000, occurred in 1976. It should be stressed, however, that Rhodesia's reduced attractiveness to whites is more clearly correlated with terrorism and military involvement than with the impact of sanctions.

Conclusions

The sanctions promulgated against Rhodesia have, with the exception of 1966, been unable to stop economic growth in that country, although without a doubt they have reduced growth below its potential. At the time sanctions were imposed, the Rhodesian economy had reached a level of sophistication and productive capabilities that allowed successful import substitution and relative ease of adjustment to boycott-induced problems. Three of the four cost categories presented were relevant to the Rhodesian embargo. Direct costs in terms of higher transport and middlemen expenses, lost tobacco revenues, and unemployment in the export sector were abundantly in evidence. Indirect costs, such as unemployment in nontrade sectors resulting from the negative multiplier effects of reduced activity in the export sector, were most visible in 1966 and tended to dissipate fairly quickly after that year. Other costs, such as quality deterioration, have lingered for years. Also included in this category are the storage and warehousing costs involved in stockpiling imported oil and subsidizing the tobacco farmers. Capital effects were only rarely in evidence and presented no serious problems. The import of spare parts and vital raw materials, particularly from South Africa, was made possible by loopholes in sanctions, and thus eliminated this cost category as a problem area. Foregone potential costs are undoubtedly enormous. Growth in tobacco and tourist revenues was assured, as was foreign investment. These potentials have gone unfulfilled, as have economies of scale that were not realized when Rhodesia's markets began to wither.

Sanctions interrupted Rhodesia's economic recovery and delayed the beginning of a period of vigorous and sustained economic growth. The major limiting aspect of sanctions in the Rhodesian case seems to lie in the reduction of export revenues. Imports have been obtainable, despite sanctions, as long as the foreign exchange has been available. It must also be stressed that Rhodesia would have been unable to survive sanctions without enormous gaps in its enforcement. A truly universal embargo, one without loopholes, would have brought quick capitulation. It is, however, unlikely that such a complete isolation can be implemented. The Rhodesian situation provides a clear reminder that trade is a two-way street. Zambia, Great Britain, Mozambique, and other African states have incurred significant costs. Even the United States has borne some costs, and it is reported that the U.S. State Department began discreetly urging the acceptance of steel imports, regardless of whether they contained Rhodesian chrome, shortly after the Byrd amendment (which had excepted chrome from American sanctions efforts) was repealed in March 1977. Because there can be significant costs to the boycotting states, it is likely that loopholes will appear in all sanctions.

It is also clear that the domestic incidence of sanctions depends not only upon the structure of the target economy but also upon the actions of the domestic political authorities, a variable beyond the control of the boycott initiators. Ian Smith has shown himself to be a skilled politician. By adroitly augmenting and manipulating governmental powers, he disarmed influential sectors that considered capitulation. The domestic impact of sanctions fell upon those with the least political clout.

Negotiations between the Smith government and a number of local African leaders, and between Smith and Anglo-American diplomats and officials of surrounding African nations, became more earnest in 1977-78. The mounting costs of guerrilla warfare, the greater militancy of surrounding states, the increase in Cuban and Soviet influence, and a number of other factors have forced Smith to accept the principle of majority rule. Sanctions continue, but it is these other factors (coupled with pressure from South Africa) that have brought about this dramatic change in the Rhodesian position. An internal settlement was drawn up in early March 1978 and signed later in the month by Ian Smith and three moderate local African leaders, Bishop Abel Muzorewa, Rev. Ndabaningi Sithole, and Chief Jeremiah Chirau. The agreement officially formed a four-man executive council to govern during the transition to majority rule, set for the end of 1978. Negotiations have been made more difficult by the existence of the Patriotic Front, a Marxist-oriented, externally based terrorist group purporting to be the sole representative of Rhodesian blacks. The Patriotic Front refuses to recognize the other black leaders, while Smith has refused to deal directly with them. Further, despite former U.S. Secretary of State Henry Kissinger's 1976 pledge that the United States would not deal directly with liberation movements in Southern Africa,[73] President Carter's administration has rejected the March accord as inadequate because it did not include either of the externally based guerrilla leaders, Joshua Nkomo and Robert Mugabe. Carter's secretary of state, Cyrus Vance, ruled out Rhodesia's request for American help to end sanctions, labeling the interim agreement a mere "proposal".[74] It remains to be seen whether majority rule will actually be instituted, whether the guerrilla leaders will lend support to the new government or wage warfare against it, and whether the United Nations will choose to lift sanctions in response to the new internal political order.

6

A Consideration of Boycotts

Economic sanctions are trade and financial penalties inflicted by boycotting states for the purpose of coercing the target nation(s) to comply with the desired ends of the boycott initiators. As such, boycotts may be selective and cover only specified commodities, such as sugar initially in the Cuban situation and tobacco originally in the Rhodesian case, or they may be general. Political success has not been forthcoming in any of the embargoes studied, despite sanctions having some very damaging economic results. This same lack of success also characterized embargoes under the auspices of the League of Nations. The nature of economic sanctions and their relation to the general field of international trade theory must be carefully considered to discover the reasons for failure, predict sanctions repercussions, and indicate weaknesses or oversights involved in their implementation or the expectations of the initiators.

The basic theory behind economic sanctions—which represent a method of coercion without resort to armed force—is that sufficient economic pressure upon the target nation(s) can induce or compel that country to more acceptable behavior in the eyes of the boycotting states. Participation in international trade has a positive real income effect that allows the consumption possibilities frontier to move beyond the domestic production curve; however, any forced diminution or withdrawal from trade will tend to reduce income. The consumption possibilities curve will move inward toward the domestic production frontier, while at the same time the actual operating point of the economy will also tend to move inward due to unemployment of both human and nonhuman factors. In addition, some of the existing capital stock may be rendered useless or ineffective by capital effects. When this is the

124

case, as it has clearly been in Cuba, then the domestic production possibilities curve itself moves inward in addition to the above factors.

The costs inflicted by economic sanctions may be either direct, indirect, foregone potential costs, capital effects, or most likely, a combination of these. Rising transport costs are perhaps the best example of direct costs, while the indirect ones include the many domestic dislocations and slowdowns that result from a disruption of normal foreign trade. Foregone potential costs include foregone export earnings from commodity or service exports and other opportunities unrealized. The foregone potential costs may possibly outweigh both the direct and indirect costs combined, but they are very difficult, if not impossible, to quantify. More important, these costs are not likely to bring about the desired political ends since opportunities foregone are only rarely missed. More immediate pressure comes from the direct and indirect expenses that can be clearly seen, both by politicians and citizens.

If sanctions are to be successful, the direct and indirect costs must be made to soar. The direct and indirect costs to Cuba were clearly the greatest of the three boycotts under study and loomed large relative to the Cuban economy. Further, capital effects were staggering, and significant opportunity costs, such as rising tourist revenues, were foregone. Despite the very high degree of effectiveness, the boycott has nevertheless been unsuccessful in producing its political ends. Rhodesia has experienced significant direct and indirect costs, but hardly comparable with the dislocations in Cuba. The opportunity costs of diminished growth in foreign investment, foregone tobacco revenues, and so forth, have no doubt been important, possibly outweighing the direct and indirect costs combined. In the Israeli situation the major impact has been in terms of foregone potential, which has been considerable, while the direct and indirect costs have been of only marginal significance.

It is obvious, then, that for boycotts to be successful politically they must be effective—economic hardship must be inflicted upon the target nation. Economic effectiveness, however, is only a necessary condition for success, not a sufficient one. Less than three million Israeli's hold out against the economic warfare of more than 100 million Arabs. Nine million Cubans have been able to withstand their economic isolation by the vast majority of

Western Hemisphere nations, while less than 300,000 Rhodesian whites have prevailed for more than a decade against economic measures launched on a global scale by the United Nations.

Further, this study suggests that partial sanctions, covering only some goods while allowing other to be exchanged, have no hope for success. In the first place, as soon as sanctions are allowed to be selective rather than comprehensive, a debate ensues concerning which items are to be allowed and which embargoed. Resolution of this controversy among the boycotting nations is likely to accommodate some boycotting states' loss minimization goals rather than a damage maximization effort toward the target nation. Second, having once decided the extent of the embargo, effective policing of such a boycott effort is almost impossible. Smuggling and clandestine trade can occur under any kind of embargo, but avoiding detection is much easier when sanctions are partial. Leonard Kapungu, for example, reports that in 1967 Rhodesia "was able to export to Italy $90,000 worth of its embargoed tobacco under the label 'eggs,'"[1] a nonembargoed item. With selective sanctions, pervasive efforts at false labeling would be expected. The policing costs of such an embargo would be staggering, and fully effective enforcement is unlikely ever to occur.

A second conclusion of this study is that embargoes against countries with large, relatively affluent economies are not likely to succeed. Larger economies, in the first place, have less recourse to international trade and are therefore less vulnerable. Their large populations tend to allow a greater division of labor and specialization within their boundaries; scale of market is already sizable and may not require expansion through trade. Further, being important suppliers and/or buyers on world markets, the imposition of sanctions against them probably would entail costs so serious to some of the imposing states that clandestine trade or open boycott contravention would occur.

The use of trade sanctions immediately changes the economic situation in a boycotted country. The target nation(s) can be expected to take steps to minimize the boycott's impact. One of these is probably going to be domestic diversification and import substitution. If infant industry potential exists, the boycott may bring about an improvement in real output in certain areas of the target economy, thereby acting as an offset to the negative income effects. This appears to be true in Rhodesia in certain sectors.

Import substitution may even be possible over a broad spectrum of goods, depending upon the adaptability and sophistication of the target economy. However, costs tend to rise (even when infant industry potential exists), and these are likely to spread to the rest of the economy. In addition, in the short-run import substitution often requires a large volume of imports at a time when the economy can ill afford foreign exchange expenditures. A hurried import substitution also tends to lower quality of output, as has been markedly noticeable both in Cuba and Rhodesia, although less so in the latter.

Another possibility is the restructuring of trade patterns so that foreign substitutes—both markets and supply sources—may be procured. This has obviously been the case in all three of the boycotts under study. Such a restructuring of trade patterns tends to worsen the terms of the trade (in addition to added transport expense). It is possible, however, that trade diversion might improve the terms of commerce by creating more optimal patterns. Thus, it could be alleged that Cuba was historically tied to a high-cost producer and the severance of this tie would have beneficial long-run effects. In point of fact, however, except for some marginal areas, this has not been the case in any of the three boycotts studied. Therefore, it seems reasonable to conclude that forced trade diversion adversely affects the terms of trade, although the exact extent depends upon the variety of other factors such as conditions in world markets, the number of nonboycotting states for which trade potential exists, and related factors. In addition, economic aid may be forthcoming from political rivals of the boycotting states, in which case the terms of trade may not move adversely.

There are other measures that can be taken to mitigate the impact of economic sanctions. Make-work projects and subsidized import substitution will tend to minimize unemployment resulting from a decrease in the foreign trade sector. At the same time, an increase in willingness to save will tend to forestall or minimize inflationary pressures deriving from the falling volume of imports coupled with increasing domestic costs and price pressures from make-work activities.

In addition, the domestic impact of sanctions is not always controllable by imposing states. As Galtung has suggested, the "collective nature of economic sanctions makes them hit the innocent along with the guilty."[2] Thus, in the Rhodesian case the effect has been shifted largely to the African population rather than falling upon the various segments of the white power structure as intended. In Cuba the incidence ultimately fell in large measure upon the middle classes, but the political situation made it impossible for any groups harmed to bring about the changes that the boycott initiators wished. The costs of trade disruption may also be borne by the boycotting states themselves and by third parties, a point to be discussed shortly.

Finally, another response to the imposition of sanctions is a conditioned adaptation to self-sacrifice. If goods cannot be produced or can only be obtained at exorbitant costs, the nation may simply adjust to the new situation and alter its life accordingly (assuming that the absolutely vital imports are maintained), rather than capitulate. When the League of Nations imposed sanctions against Italy, Mussolini exhorted his countrymen to do without for the protection and safety of their country. Castro, of course, has done the same. Indeed, sacrifice becomes a national campaign. In fact, even examples of conspicuous sacrifice—such as the media's depicting Ian Smith conserving petrol by using a bicycle rather than his car—will be found.

Sanctions have thus far been unsuccessful in each of the cases studied, despite the target economies being relatively small and highly vulnerable. For sanctions to be successful, however, the economic damage inflicted must be sufficient to unleash domestic political pressures that will either topple an intransigent regime or bring about the adoption of new policies more in accord with the norms of the boycotting nations. Success or failure, then, rests not only upon the degree of economic hardships inflicted but basically upon the internal impact of sanctions, the nature of the domestic political system, and the attitude of the target population.

"Clearly, if political disintegration should take place it would happen through the dual effect of sanctions, which weakens the people in power and strengthens those in opposition."[3] Yet the boycotts of both Rhodesia and Cuba have been used by the regimes as an excuse to extend certain powers. Given the strong degree of personal control Castro exercises in Cuba, the erosion of his political position seems unlikely. The Cuban government controls almost all information flows and at the same time has taken very effective measures to stifle opposition groups, so the damages wrought by the boycott have neither weakened Castro's domestic position nor stimulated the creation of an effective political opposition. Moreover, the internal incidence of sanctions fell largely upon the Cuban middle and upper classes. The upper-income groups have left the island, as have many of the middle class. Those remaining—many engaged in small retail or manufacturing activities—were particularly harmed by the embargo, and their economic power was nullified by the many nationalizations that occurred. Cuban peasants and the urban poor were in such dire economic shape before the embargo that continuing hardship was nothing new. Moreover, wealth confiscations and subsequent redistributions mitigated the impact upon the peasantry. Finally, the regime's control of almost all information media has enabled them to depict the "imperialist blockade" as the cause of many domestic problems. A Cuban self-image has been created that depicts Castro and his country as courageously marching forward and prevailing in spite of the economic aggression of the United States. Exhortations to greater achievements and further sacrifice—commonplace in the motivational propaganda of socialist states—have thus been reinforced by "imperialist economic warfare."

In the Rhodesian situation a much more fluid political environment prevailed before sanctions, with free elections having been held and meaningful opposition groups existing. In the face of sanctions, however, the Smith regime has been able effectively to minimize opposition. One major reason for continued Rhodesian intransigence is that most of the internal effect of sanctions fell mainly upon the "wrong" group—the African population which wielded no political power. The largest economic group within the electorate, white employees, emerged virtually unscathed during 1966, the most damaging year of sanctions. Their position was protected by adroit governmental policies to minimize white unemployment. Sanctions losses also fell heavily upon impersonal groups (corporate profits) and upon incorporated small establishments, particularly in the retail trades. White employees have endured only minor hardships and have placed few pressures upon the regime. Tobacco farmers, on the other hand, although hit hardest economically by sanctions, have been among the most ardent supporters of UDI and are thus ideologically commited to the political course being followed.

The initiators of economic sanctions generally overlook the potential for adaptive adjustments within the target states, both economic and otherwise. Indeed, political integration rather than disintegration is likely if the ruling elite responds to sanctions with sagacious defensive policies. The attitude of the population becomes very important in assessing sanctions. If the boycotts can be depicted as attacks from the outside upon the group as a whole, or upon its way of life, resistance will be strong. If there is weak identification with the attacker(s), this too will reinforce resistance on the part of the populace. And if no other acceptable alternatives can be found, life under sanctions will remain preferable to capitulation. In the Cuban situation the boycott has been depicted as aggression not against Castro but against the entire nation and its aspirations. Resistance is bolstered by playing upon an historic resentment against the "colossus to the North." Finally, the superiority of the Cuban socialist system being created—as opposed to the brutal and inhumane system of American capitalism—has been stressed as preferable to a Cuba again under American suzerainty.

The same strategy and factors are at work in Rhodesia. The attack is pictured as one upon the entire group and its way of life, launched by an external force misguided in direction and goals. Resistance becomes synonomous with patriotism, while dissent becomes treason. Indeed, Rhodesian whites have been inundated with cries of Communist conspiracy and have seemed often ready to believe such opinions in order to rationalize their actions. It has become common to hear that former British prime minister Harold Wilson was really a Communist, that it has been the Communists who most sincerely wish to destroy Rhodesia and who have led and prodded the African states and Britain to initiate the unjust sanctions. White Rhodesians see themselves as the underdog resisting this world-wide conspiracy and struggling to open the eyes of those who unknowingly are assisting Communist aggression. These views have undoubtedly been given greater credence by the recent ascendancy of leftist regimes in Mozambique and Angola. Finally, the government has depicted capitulation as more than simply a return to pre-UDI conditions. The prospect of rapid enfranchisement of the largely uneducated African majority, under the sway of ruthless demagogues, evokes visions of the blood bath in the Congo. The frequent breakdowns in negotiations and years of frustration have now made the one-man, one-vote principle and its immediate introduction an inexorable demand of the many factions allegedly representing the African majority. Faced with this frightening alternative, the European population's resistance has stiffened.

It is clear that the amount of sacrifice and the extent of adaptation a nation will endure is a highly significant factor. Leadership attitudes are also important in this regard. Cuba is a good case in point. Castro has been actively seeking the support of U.S. business leaders to end the embargo. President Carter has repeatedly indicated that if Cuba reduces its involvement in Africa, he would move toward restored relations. Yet Castro's African intervention has increased and not only is maintained in Angola but currently reaches into Algeria, Mozambique, Somalia, and elsewhere. U.S. State Department estimates of Cuban troop strength in Africa have been increased to 30,000, although a 50,000 figure may be closer to the mark.[4] Castro's African policy clearly runs directly counter to Carter's. The cost to Cuba of continuing the embargo is significant and one Castro obviously recognizes. Yet it is one he apparently is willing to have Cuba bear.

In the Israeli case the boycott inflicted only marginal damage. Its area of greatest impact probably is that of foregone potential. Opportunities unrealized, however, will not evoke the political pressures that strong direct and indirect costs would. More important, the attitude of the Israeli population is such that capitulation is unthinkable even if sanctions were highly effective. The Arab states have not recognized Israel's right to exist, so it is not so much a change of policy or government that has been sought, but rather the destruction of the nation as a political entity. Given this goal, Israel must of necessity totally reject capitulation regardless of actual or potential damage. Powerful factors are present in the Israeli situation, then, that solidify resistance: the attack is upon the entire nation, by parties with whom almost absolute negative identification exists, coupled with the total absence of an acceptable alternative. To sum, if the attitude of the population can be guided or molded into defensive patterns of thinking, frequently not a difficult task, sanctions will cause neither political disintegration nor capitulation. Indeed, sanctions are likely to further the legitimacy of the target state regime and its offending actions.

A final, speculative exercise concerning the attitude of the population raises important issues. Participation in the Vietnam war was vigorously opposed by many vocal elements within the United States. At the United Nations and at other world forums American involvement was vehemently condemned. It might be asked, what would have occurred within the United States if the United Nations had imposed economic sanctions in order to force American disengagement? Foreign condemnation of American actions seemed to lend very little support to the efforts of American "doves," hence such sanctions would probably also have given the dove effort little momentum. Sanctions, on the other hand, might have had some rather perverse impacts, at least from the perspective of the initiators. Might they not have been viewed as an attack upon the nation, launched from the outside by a conspiracy of nonwestern, undemocratic, Communist and third-world nations seeking to undermine American affluence, world influence, and the American way of life? A rampant "yellow journalism" could have played up those themes, and in such an atmosphere the nation probably would be converted into "hawks." Of course, there never was any likelihood of such sanctions; however, this speculative scenario is within the realm of reason and does emphasize the role and importance of the attitude of the population.

This study of politically motivated trade cessations has indirectly argued the case for international trade and the concomitant benefits by looking at exceptions—situations in which trade is artificially constrained by embargoes. It is clear that the gains from voluntary trade are mutual and that imports tend to keep domestic price levels from rising. In addition, quality of output is likely to suffer considerably if import substitution that ignores comparative advantage is undertaken. Finally, the findings emphasize that the benefits from trade essentially derive from imports rather than exports, a basic but often overlooked point. To refuse to purchase another country's exports harms that nation by depriving it of the purchasing power necessary to procure foreign supplies. Negative employment and income effects of reduced exports can generally be offset by government countermeasures; however, governments are ordinarily unable to command foreign goods or supplies without foreign currency. This suggests that effective sanctions must be import-oriented, that is, supplies of goods to the target nation should be cut off as quickly and as completely as possible if the boycotting states wish the sanctions to have a meaningful impact. To achieve this end, however, naval blockades and military actions in support of the embargo may be necessary.

Loopholes in sanctions enforcement are important consid- erations. In none of the boycotts studied have sanctions completely stifled the target economy's international trade. Significant and glaring gaps in Rhodesian sanctions have enabled that nation to survive and prosper. In their absence, however, the economy would have quickly withered. Loopholes take the form of open noncompliance, as with South Africa and Mexico (which never severed its Cuban trade), or various forms of clandestine trade, including direct contacts between boycotting and target economies through smuggling. Regarding the inability of sanctions to extinguish trade, the almost identical comments of two merchants of different nationalities, at different times, are illuminating. A New York importer-exporter, in response to the author's 1969 survey, wrote that embargoes never operate very effectively. He volunteered that the sanctions against Rhodesia "are a farce." Almost nine years later a South African executive, after describing the extent of South Africa's "backdoor trade," also labeled Rhodesian sanctions a "farce."[5]

The economic effectiveness of sanctions is also a function of the demand for the products of the boycotting states. The more inelastic the demand for embargoed imports, the greater the damage rendered. If the boycotting states supply consumption or production necessities for which import substitution is difficult or impossible, the target economy will absorb considerable economic losses. Single-use items, such as specially designed equipment, spare parts, or specific forms of raw materials, tend to have inelastic demands. Cuba was particularly harmed in this regard, suffering significant capital effects. If, on the other hand, import substitution is not inordinately difficult or if alternate foreign suppliers are available, the demand for embargoed items will be more elastic and the problems caused will be less significant. Finally, the time period involved is an important variable. In relatively short periods demand tends to be less elastic. As time passes, however, new processes embodying fewer imports may be introduced, synthetics or economizing may lessen demand for foreign raw materials, and many other adjustments can be introduced. This suggests that boycotts are most effective in the short-run when dependence upon the goods previously supplied externally is still strong, but enough time has not elapsed for successful adaptive measures.

In addition to a reduction in economic effectiveness over time, it is probable that the boycotting states themselves may weary of their efforts and the failure of their designs. Certainly this was the League of Nations' experience. Kapungu holds that the "longer economic sanctions take to be effective the less they are likely to continue to receive international support. The international public tends to lose interest in a crisis that drags on indefinitely."[6] By the second half of the 1960s there was mounting evidence of a movement within the United States to end the Cuban embargo. Indeed, one plank in the Eugene McCarthy platform for the Democratic party's presidential nomination in 1968 was restoration of trade and normal commerce with Cuba. This trend continued and strengthened in the early 1970s, and the United States applied no pressure upon its Western Hemisphere allies to continue sanctions when the Organization of American States met in July 1975. Despite O.A.S. policy changes, the United States ban on direct trade, with modifications, continues.

One such modification, an important one, was termination of the ban on tourist travel in 1977. It can be expected (and is certainly hoped for by Cuban officials) that increasing numbers of American tourists will visit the island. Such exchanges are likely to create additional pressures for normalization of trade and commerce. Further, interest mounts within the American business community to end the boycott. "Why should the Canadians be getting business I could be getting?" one New England businessman asked.[7] This sentiment is spreading. Although President Carter has declared that a reduced African involvement is the price Castro must pay to end the embargo, Castro has thus far ignored Carter's wishes. The inefficacy of the embargo to control or influence Castro casts further suspicion on its usefulness. Indeed, it may well be that Castro himself realizes (or believes) that the embargo will probably be discarded before too long, even if he does not modify his foreign policy. If so, he can safely ignore Carter's warnings, knowing that time is on his side.[8]

Another possible consequence of boycotts is emigration. Economic hardships arising from sanctions may contribute to emigration if the quality of life deteriorates sufficiently. An exodus of people, in turn, may exacerbate economic difficulties and place strong pressure for change upon the government. In two of the three cases studied, however, this possibility does not appear to be relevant. For Israelis, there are few places to go. The older generation, not native born, emigrated from lands considered to be hostile to Jews, to settle in a Jewish state. The younger generations have been born on Israeli soil and have no past "homelands" and little inclination to leave. What emigration there has been is relatively small and generally by recent immigrants who found the Israeli way of life unsuitable. It is highly unlikely that the boycott plays any role in a decision to emigrate, although the same cannot be said for guerrilla and terrorist activities. In the Cuban situation there was substantial emigration because of a variety of factors, including the open-door policy of the United States toward Cuban immigrants, Castro's radicalism and attacks on the traditional Cuban socioeconomic system, and political persecutions. After Castro consolidated his power, substantial emigration was precluded. Hence, even if boycott-induced economic hardship would have caused population loss, the political situation prevented this.

The emigration possibility, however, is quite relevant to Rhodesia. European unemployment or depressed incomes could stimulate migrations to neighboring South Africa or, perhaps, to other Commonwealth lands. The average white Rhodesian income in 1965, however, was roughly 25 percent higher than the corresponding figure for South Africa. If emigration based upon economic considerations alone were to occur, this gap would have to narrow substantially and it has not. Further, the costs of moving and the probable loss of wealth from forced sales would be additional considerations tending to minimize emigration, even if average incomes were equalized. Rather than mass exodus, however, Rhodesia has been able to attract settlers, gaining almost 12,500 as late as 1975. Nevertheless, emigration began to be significant in 1973, and 1976 witnessed the first net loss of Europeans, some 7,000, since 1966. It appears that net losses occurred in 1977 as well. It should be recalled that during 1961–64, a politically unsettled period (accompanied by rioting and some bloodshed) when the Federation was dissolving, Rhodesia overcame the loss of 25,000 Europeans. Stagnation and economic declines accompanied the exodus, but real growth resumed shortly after the political uncertainties cleared. The probable cause of the recent changes in migration patterns lies not with sanctions, but with increases in guerrilla activities, terrorism and the concommitant Rhodesian troop call-ups, loss of life, and increased taxes to pay for the defense burden.

The step up in guerrilla activities and armed incursions both in Israel and Rhodesia reflects the frustration of those imposing sanctions (or siding with them) with the political ineffectiveness of embargoes. When boycotts, presumably nonmilitary methods of coercion, fail to achieve their objectives, they tend either to be abandoned or the frustrations engendered lead to activities that substitute violence for economic pressures. These latter activities have very pronounced economic impacts, including reducing tourism and foreign investment revenues, discouraging immigration and encouraging emigration, requiring an increased proportion of the national product to be devoted to defense activities, and so forth. The imminent downfall of the white government in Rhodesia, if it occurs, will be the result of armed conflict rather than sanctions. Interestingly, it is possible that Cuban troops or military advisers may play a key role in such a conflict. Considering that one of the initial reasons alleged for sanctions against Cuba was to make the export of revolution more difficult, Cuban involvement in African upheavals is ironic testimony to the failure of those sanctions.

Insight into one aspect of multilateral boycotts can be gained by viewing embargoes from the perspective of theories of collusion usually applied to oligopoly markets. Sanctions may be viewed as overt collusive arrangements. As such, the greater the number of boycotting states, the more likely it is that secret cheating will occur (although it may still be true that the larger the number of enforcing countries, the more effective the embargo). A study of sanctions clearly brings to the fore the mutually beneficial nature of voluntary exchange. Covert trade is likely not only because with more boycotting states detection of non-cooperation is more difficult, but essentially because it is economically advantageous, even if not morally acceptable. The U.S. Congress passed the Byrd Amendment, which allowed the importation of Rhodesian chrome, because Rhodesian supplies were deemed important and necessary to American interests. It was apparently felt that continued imposition of sanctions, with no exceptions, was deleterious to the United States.[9] In late April 1976 the stockholders of the Union Carbide Corporation rejected a stockholder proposal that would have barred the company from importing Rhodesian chrome ore until international sanctions were lifted. The stockholders apparently felt that trade with Rhodesia was too profitable to forego. At that same meeting the stockholders defeated a proposal that would have required the directors to provide a full report on the company's policy toward the Arab boycott. The Union Carbide management had opposed both proposals.

Hence, it is evident that sanctions can rarely be "imposed" upon others without the boycotting states themselves suffering various degrees of losses. Indeed, Rhodesia's staunchest political foe, Zambia, found it impossible to sever trade relations completely and simply tapered them off (with external assistance) as much as it could. Since 1970 the number of evasion cases detected and reported by the United Nations Sanctions Committee has increased substantially. It appears that enforcement efforts and compliance have waned considerably since the "crisis" became permanent. In the Arab world Jordan undoubtably suffers considerale economic harm, both in terms of transit fees and joint use of irrigation and other projects that have been foregone, and in terms of higher transport costs from rerouting its trade away from the Israeli port of Haifa, Jordan's natural outlet to the sea, to Beirut via Damascus—an awkward and relatively expensive trip. Indeed, the uneven incidence of embargoes explains why many Arab states have chosen to ignore the Israeli boycott regulations when this proved advantageous. It is interesting that the more effective sanctions are in imparting economic damage, the more likely boycott contravention becomes. The target state is denied needed products, whose value there increases substantially, and thereby becomes more willing to pay higher prices; this in turn increases the boycotting states' costs of refusing to sell.

Sanctions bring costs not only to the nations directly involved but may also affect third-party states. Further, the effect of sanctions may be shifted internationally. As stated, Zambia received external assistance when it began reducing its trade with Rhodesia. This meant that the cost of imposing sanctions was partially shifted from Zambia to those nations aiding it. Mozambique, when it closed the border with Rhodesia, was promised aid to ameliorate the costs of imposing sanctions. Here again an international shifting of incidence occurs. In Israel contributions from world Jewry aid the state and the burden of the boycott is reduced. It could, perhaps, be claimed that the incidence of the boycott is partially shifted to world Jewry; however such contributions would have been forthcoming regardless of the embargo. If the size of this extra assistance is related to Arab activities, it is not the boycott, but the state of military hostilities, that is the crucial variable. Hence, it is the costs of national defense rather than the boycott that are partially shifted. In the Cuban case the Soviet Union and other bloc states have extended aid as a direct consequence of Cuba's economic isolation. Here, then, is a clear example of international shifting to third-party states, political allies of the target nation. Hence, the Soviet and East European consumer (assuming the aid derived from resources that otherwise would have produced consumer goods) has borne some portion of the costs of the embargo against Cuba! Indeed, as early as 1963 it was reported that "this burden is being felt, especially in bloc countries like Czechoslovakia which has assumed a major portion of this load."[10]

The involvement of third parties can place strains upon international alliances. In the case of the Cuban embargo, for example, the United States applied pressure upon Canada and its European allies to cease trade with Cuba. Further, American companies in these lands came under dual and conflicting jurisdictions, being governed by the U.S. Export Control Act, yet subject to the laws of the host countries, which were not boycotting Cuba. Exporting goods to Cuba by American companies or subsidiaries was contrary to the Export Control Act, yet refusal to take advantage of trade opportunities has been deemed by the host countries to be contrary to their best interests. American pressure upon foreign governments and upon U.S. overseas subsidiaries has been rather coldly received in most Western capitals, and relations between the United States and its allies became mildly strained over this issue.

Economic sanctions could be rendered considerably more effective and far more likely to achieve their political goals if they were supported by the necessary police actions. Such actions would be confined to blocking access, by land and sea, to and from the target state. If the Arab nations, for example, which already control all land and pipeline routes to Israel, were to blockade Israeli ports, the economic consequences would probably prove disastrous. Were the United States to use naval forces to isolate Cuba completely from its trade partners, the economy would grind to a complete halt. However, there are serious problems involved in such actions. First, such activities would require military or naval support and thus eliminate the pacific, or nonmilitary, nature of the original method of coercion. There is little question that an attempted Arab naval blockade would move the conflict from the economic sphere to the military one. Indeed, the attempt to close the Straits of Tiran—Israel's window to the East—was a contributing cause of the Six-Day War of 1967.

A second, yet related problem, concerns the serious political and military dangers involved when third-party states are affected by the boycotting nations' police actions. Consider, for example, the political consequences of American warships detaining Soviet commercial vessels, or perhaps, sinking such vessels if they refused to stop or be boarded. What if the Soviets provided armed naval support for their commercial vessels dealing with Cuba? Could the United States continue to enforce a blockade without serious risk of starting a third world war? It is an internationally legitimate exercise of sovereignty for one nation to desist from trade with another. For a nation, however, to insist by means of force that some other state not trade with the target country, a nation not at war with the sanctions-imposing state, is a clear infraction of the third-party state's sovereignty and may indeed precipitate conflict.

The costs of economic sanctions in the three cases studied differ in degree and kind, yet in none of the target economies have economic hardships led directly to the political changes envisioned by those imposing sanctions. This study suggests that boycotts are most likely to be successful in the short-run, when their economic effectiveness tends to be greatest. However, economic effectiveness in no way guarantees the desired political outcomes. Economic damage is a necessary condition for success, but not a sufficient one. Less than three million Israelis hold out against the economic warfare of more than 100 million Arabs. Nine million

Cubans have been able to withstand their economic isolation by the vast majority of Western Hemisphere nations, while less than 300,000 Rhodesian whites have prevailed for more than a decade against economic measures launched on a global scale by the United Nations. The three boycotts studied have thus far failed to accomplish their political ends, and it seems unlikely that economic measures alone will fare better in the future.

Notes

Chapter 1

1. For a concise account of the economic impact of blockades, see François Crouzet, "Wars, Blockades and Economic Change in Europe, 1797–1815," *Journal of Economic History*, December 1964, pp. 567-88.

2. The term *boycott* is used here to refer only to international economic boycotts and not to those used in strictly domestic affairs. Although economic *sanctions* are sometimes considered official acts, with *boycotts* being considered unofficial undertakings by private parties, the terms *sanction, boycott,* and *embargo* will be used interchangeably.

3. Charles F. Remer, *A Study of Chinese Boycotts* (Baltimore: John Hopkins Press, 1933).

4. J. F. Dulles, "Practicable Sanctions," in *Boycotts and Peace: Report by the Committee on Economic Sanctions,* ed. Evans Clark (New York: Harper and Brothers, 1932), p. 18. Dulles was here referring to collective sanctions rather than individual.

5. Ibid., p. 21

6. Edwin C. Eckel, "General Conclusions and Recommendations," in Clark, ed., p. 257.

7. J. Whitton and M. Gonsiorowski, "Sanctions," in Clark, ed., p. 95.

8. For an interesting account of the sanctions against Italy, see Herbert Feis, *Three International Episodes: Seen from E.A.* (New York: W. W. Norton and Company, 1966), pp. 193-294.

9. Margaret P. Doxey, *Economic Sanctions and International Enforcement* (New York: Oxford University Press, 1971), p. 11.

Chapter 2

1. See R. Harrod, *International Economics,* rev. ed. (Chicago: University of Chicago Press, 1958), p. 3.

2. Gerald M. Meier, *International Trade and Development* (New York: Harper and Row, 1963), p. 18.

3. Harrod, *International Economics,* pp. 12-38.

4. See Murray Kemp, "The Gain from International Trade," *Economic Journal,* December 1962, p. 808.

5. See H. Linneman, *An Econometric Study of International Trade Flows* (Amsterdam: North Holland Publishing Company, 1966). Of course, distance in statute miles is not as important as the economic cost of transportation. A relatively short geographical distance may be economically "long" if the terrain is difficult to traverse or there are other encumbrances entailing added expenses.

6. Leland Yeager and David Tuerck, *Trade Policy and the Price System* (Scranton, Pa.: International Textbook Company, 1966), p. 62.

7. For an enlightening account of the relationship between achievement motivation and economic development, see David McClelland, *The Achieving Society* (Princeton, N.J.: Van Nostrand, 1961). It should be noted that political stability is a condition for economic development. To the extent that growing aspirations are unmatched by (or outstrip)

accomplishments, rising frustrations result, possibly leading to political instability, which retards economic growth.

8. Yeager and Tuerck, *Trade Policy*, p. 37.

9. Harrod, *International Economics*, p. 43.

10. Jan Pen, *A Primer on International Trade* (New York: Vintage Books, 1967), p. 38.

11. The fact that Israel has reduced its foreign exchange outlays by establishing its own merchant marine does not remove the element of cost—resources thereby committed become unavailable for more productive alternatives.

12. The fact that Cuba has received bloc aid since its break with the United States does not remove this element of direct cost. Additional transport expenses were still created but subsidized. Thus, the target nation has been able to shift a portion of the boycott's incidence to third-party states.

13. See Franklyn D. Holzman, "Import Bottlenecks and the Foreign Trade Multiplier," *Western Economic Journal*, June 1969, pp. 101-8.

14. The cost of such facilities together with losses on sales effected for 1966 and 1967 was £34 million. See "Rhodesia," *Standard Bank Review*, August 1968, p. 16.

15. Despite the inconveniences and extra expenses of the boycott, Israel's tourist industry has prospered. No doubt a greater harmful influence since 1967 has been the state of half-war and Arab guerrilla activities.

16. See Carmelo Mesa-Lago, "Availability and Reliability of Statistics in Socialist Cuba," *Latin American Research Review*, Spring and Summer 1969, pp. 53-92, 47-82.

17. A. M. Hawkins, "The Rhodesian Economy under Sanctions," *Rhodesian Journal of Economics*, August 1967, p. 46.

18. K. Miyazawa, "Foreign Trade Multiplier, Input-Output Analysis and the Consumption Function," *Quarterly Journal of Economics*, February 1960, pp. 53-64.

19. If imports were $15 rather than $10, sanctions would not be neutral, but would raise net money income by $10 (although real income must fall somewhat due to nonparticipation in trade).

20. Holzman, "Import Bottlenecks," pp. 104-7.

21. The inability to obtain necessary spare parts—technical necessities, although not always normally of great value—can bring entire production systems to a halt. A small filter worth roughly $25 jeopardized the entire operations of a major Cuban nickel plant. Indeed, the parts systems throughout Cuban mines, factories, and electrical and telephone systems all depended upon American supplies. The embargo caused innumerable breakdowns and severely damaged the transportation system. Neither socialist bloc substitutes not domestic ones proved satisfactory.

22. Hal B. Lary, *Imports of Manufactures from Less Developed Countries* (New York: National Bureau of Economic Research, 1968), p. 10.

23. Perhaps "economically close" is a more appropriate term, since it is the cost of transport rather than the distance alone that is most relevant.

Chapter 3

1. Israel and Rhodesia are the only other developing nations that have experienced meaningful multilateral trade embargoes; however, in neither case was dependence upon one specific supplier and market as great as in the Cuban situation.

2. See, for example, David Barkin, "Cuban Agriculture: A Strategy of Economic Development," *Studies in Comparative International Development* vol. 7, no. 1, or Harry G. Shaffer and Stephen G. Mitchell, "Cuba: Present and Future," *Queen's Quarterly*, Summer 1972, pp. 208-224. Fidel Castro's July 26, 1970, speech presents an excellent summary of

Cuba's problems, particularly from the viewpoint of the administrative apparatus. It is reprinted in the *New York Review of Books,* 24 September 1970, pp. 18-32.

3. See Theodore Draper, *Castro's Revolution: Myths and Realities* (New York: Fredrick A. Praeger, 1962); Waldo Frank, *Cuba: Prophetic Island* (New York: Marzani and Mansell, 1961); Jules Dubois, *Fidel Castro: Rebel, Liberator or Dictator?* (Indianapolis: Bobbs-Merrill, 1959); or C. Barnet and W. MacGaffey *Cuba* (New Haven: Human Relations Area Files Press, 1962), for varied accounts of Castro as a leader and individual.

4. See Henry Wriston, "A Historical Perspective," in *Cuba and the United States,* ed. J. Plank (Washington, D.C.: Brookings Institution, 1967), pp. 1-44.

5. See Eric Baklanoff, "The Creative Impact: U.S. Business Investments and Economic Development in Cuba, 1946-1960," *Intercollegiate Review,* Fall 1968, for a summary of benefits during the 15-year period prior to Castro.

6. See Donald Losman, "International Economic Sanctions: The Boycotts of Cuba, Israel, and Rhodesia" (Ph.D. diss., University of Florida, 1969), pp. 18-28, 41-53, 84-93.

7. Data taken from both United Nations and Cuban sources. See ibid., pp. 97-100.

8. Economic Research Bureau, Inc., *Economic Intelligence Report: Cuba,* vol.2, no. 9, p. 2; and U.S. Congress, Senate, Committee on Judiciary, *Hearings on Cuban Refugee Program,* pt.3, 89th Cong., 2d sess., 1966 (Washington, D.C.: Government Printing Office), pp. 229-30.

9. See D. Losman, "Soviet Trade with Cuba: Motives, Methods, and Meaning," *Duquesne Review,* Fall 1969, pp. 127–53, and Edward González, "Castro's Revolution, Cuban Communist Appeals, and the Soviet Response," *World Politics,* October 1968, pp. 39-68.

10. For an analysis of these arrangements and their economic implications, see D. Losman, "The Economics of Bloc Aid and Trade with Cuba," *Marquette Business Review,* Summer 1970, pp. 68-77. Due to the "barter" basis of most of these agreements, the nominal figures have exaggerated the real value of socialist aid.

11. *New York Review of Books,* 24 September 1970, p. 28.

12. Estimates are based on the flat interscale rates and derived with the aid of Paul LeRoux, supply analyst, Esso Inter-America, Inc., Miami, Florida.

13. Estimate from Barber Steamship Lines, Inc., New York, New York.

14. Based on transport costs rules of thumb provided in C. P. Kindleberger, *Foreign Trade and the National Economy* (New Haven: Yale University Press, 1962), p. 12, and data presented on oil and rice transport. The estimate is considered conservative.

15. Estimate was computed as follows: 4.7 percent of the 1963 import total was taken as transport expense, assuming trade with the United States and neighbors (figure based on Kindleberger, n. 14), then multiplied by 3. This total was multiplied by .75 to account for the fact that only ¾ of imports came from the socialist bloc. This was probably not necessary because all imports came from overseas, hence the estimate is conservative on this account also. From this figure was subtracted the original amount that would likely have prevailed had trade been through traditional channels. The difference was roughly $50 million. For 1964 this figure was no doubt higher because of a greater volume of imports.

16. Quoted in "An Opening Door to Cuba," *Business Week,* 14 September 1975, p. 27.

17. *Barclay's Country Reports,* "Cuba," 25 February 1976, p. 2.

18. Edward Boorstein, *The Economic Transformation of Cuba* (New York: Monthly Review Press, 1968), p. 211.

19. Shaffer and Mitchell, "Cuba," p. 213.

20. David Lehmann, "The Trajectory of the Cuban Revolution," *Journal of Development Studies,* January 1971, p. 207.

21. K. S. Karol, *Guerrillas in Power,* trans. Arnold Pomerans (New York: Hill and Wang, 1970), p. 224.

22. "Cuba's Foreign Trade," *Panorama Económico Latino-americano* 185 (1967), p. 7.

23. For a graphic illustration of these points, see chapter 2.

24. U.S. Department of Commerce, Joint Publications Research Service, trans. no. 21233, p. 8, *El Mundo,* August 1963.

25. Boorstein, *Economic Tranformation of Cuba,* p. 59.

26. Ibid.

27. James O'Conner, "Industrial Organization in the Old and New Cubas," *Science and Society,* Spring 1966, p. 289.

28. Economist Intelligence Unit, *Cuba, Dominican Republic, Haiti, Puerto Rico: Quarterly Economic Review* 2 (1971), p. 11.

29. Boorstein, *Economic Transformation of Cuba,* p. 115.

30. Economist Intelligence Unit, *Cuba, Dominican Republic, Haiti, Puerto Rico: Quarterly Economic Review* 1 (1971), p. 9.

31. Ibid.

32. Quoted in Cuban Economic Research Project, *Stages and Problems of Industrial Development in Cuba* (Coral Gables: University of Miami Press, 1965), p. 199.

33. Economic Research Bureau, Inc., *Economic Intelligence Report: Cuba,* vol. 2, no. 11, p. 5.

34. Ibid., p. 9.

35. Carmelo Mesa-Lago, "Conversion of the Cuban Economy," *Journal of Economic Issues,* March 1974, p. 54. Mesa-Lago correctly points out that ideological biases, overambitious planning, and other factors contributed to the deterioration of sugar milling capacity. There is, however, no mention in his essay of the embargo and the mills' dependence upon American parts.

36. Lehmann, "Cuban Revolution," p. 208.

37. See Max Nolff, "Industry," in *Cuba,* ed. Dudley Seers (Chapel Hill: University of North Carolina Press, 1964), pp. 321-22.

38. With regard to the availability and reliability of statistical information, the interested reader should see Seers, *Cuba,* pp. x-xi, and Mesa-Lago, "Availability and Reliability of Statistics," pp. 53-92, 47-82.

39. The official estimate of average annual capital consumption in the 1950s was 5.9 percent. See Banco Nacional de Cuba, *Memoria 1958-1969* (Havana), p. 101.

40. The writer is aware of the difficulties and weaknesses associated with the automatic use of these figures without regard to other conditions and factors. See, for example, Joan Robinson, *Economic Philosophy* (New York: Doubleday and Company, Inc., 1962), pp. 106-11.

41. See Mesa-Lago, "Availability and Reliability of Statistics," pp. 53-92, 47-82.

42. Economist Intelligence Unit, *Cuba, Dominican Republic, Haiti, Puerto Rico: Quarterly Economic Review* 2 (1971), p. 4. Estimate uses 1965 pesos as a base. It appears that the 1968 GNP was also poor, falling below that of 1966. See Carmelo Mesa-Lago, "The Revolutionary Offensive," in *Cuban Communism,* ed. I. L. Horowitz (Transaction Books, 1970), pp. 87-88.

43. Cuba during the 1960s was hit by several rather severe hurricanes. A drought in 1967-68 was also particularly damaging to the sugar crop. For the impact of another variable, unpaid labor, see Carmelo Mesa-Lago, "Economic Significance of Unpaid Labor in Socialist Cuba," *Industrial and Labor Relations Review,* April 1969, pp. 339-57.

44. Wolfgang Stolper, "The Multiplier if Imports are for Investments," in Robert Baldwin et al., *Trade, Growth and the Balance of Payments* (Chicago: Rand McNally and Company, 1965), pp. 131-32.

45. Celso Furtado, *Development and Underdevelopment* (Berkley: University of California Press, 1967), p. 150.

46. A fourth factor influencing the quality of output, although not attributable to the boycott, would include any disincentive effects resulting from Castro's institutional rearrangements and/or resulting misallocations of resources. On the other hand, it may be

held that such rearrangements have improved incentives and resource allocation, thus raising quality. It is difficult to prove which possibility prevails.

47. Lary, *Imports of Manufacturers*, p. 10.

48. See Jack Baranson, "Transfer of Technical Knowledge by International Corporations to Developing Economies," *American Economic Review*, May 1966, pp. 259-67; and Wilfred Malenbaum, "Comparative Costs and Economic Development: The Experience of India," *American Economic Review*, May 1964, p. 396.

49. Ivan Hernandez, quoted in Don Bohning, "Shortage of Petroleum in Cuba Puts New Squeeze on a Shaky Economy," *Miami Herald*, 17 December 1967, p. 8D.

50. Quoted in Boorstein, *Economic Transformation of Cuba*, p. 106.

51. Ibid., p. 103.

52. J. Wilner Sundelson, "A Business Perspective," in *Cuba*, ed. Plank, p. 111.

53. Ibid., p. 100.

54. Boorstein, *Economic Transformation of Cuba*, p. 97.

55. Of course, these shortages are not due solely to the embargo. Many other factors contributed, but particularly important has been the increasing amount of resources devoted to investment. "Aggregate data," according to Barkin, "reflect a policy of freezing or even lowering personal consumption levels in order to divert resources to investment. . . ." ("Cuban Agriculture," p. 29). Excessive absenteeism and bureaucratic shortages have also played an important role.

56. It should be stressed that due to income redistribution measures it is likely that food consumption increased quite rapidly and would have strained Cuba's capacity even without the boycott. The embargo, of course, made conditions just that much more difficult.

57. Economist Intelligence Unit, *Cuba, Dominican Republic, Haiti, Puerto Rico: Quarterly Economic Review* 1 (1969), p. 3.

58. *World Bank Atlas*, 1973.

59. This is not to suggest that *all* internal actions and policies have been growth-retarding or deleterious to the standard of living. Indeed, at least one authority has indicated to this writer that, in his opinion, the majority of Cubans are today better off than in the pre-Castro period. This is attributed to a variety of factors, including wealth and income redistributions, provision of education and health measures, and full employment.

60. Annual repayments on the 1971 debt are estimated at $131 million. See Economist Intelligence Unit, *Cuba, Dominican Republic, Haiti, and Puerto Rico: Quarterly Economic Review* 2 (1971). In December 1972, Russia granted Cuba a thirteen year deferment on Cuba's debt payments (principal and interest).

61. No doubt its geographic separation from the bloc is also a factor. It is of interest to note the comprehensive aid agreements concluded with the Soviet Union in the early 1970s. They provide for significant participation of Soviet personnel in Cuba's planning and enterprise management. It appears that this degree of participation has impinged upon Cuban (or Castro's) autonomy. The *Wall Street Journal* (Robert Keatley, "Conflicting Goals in Castro's Cuba," 12 May 1977, p. 16) reports that "Soviet advisors have already installed a Russian-type party and government structure to restrict the free-wheeling Castro ways, and this influence grows."

62. Quoted in ibid.

63. Castro's reduction in hemisphere adventurism and his diversion of efforts to other stages has also contributed to revised policies in Latin America.

Chapter 4

1. B. Y. Boutros-Ghali, "The Arab League: Ten Years of Struggle," *International Conciliation*, May 1954, p. 421.

2. The Protocol of Alexandria was signed by Egypt, Jordan, Syria, Lebanon, Saudi Arabia, Iraq, Yemen, and delegates from the Palestinian Arabs.

3. Boutros-Ghali, "Arab League," p. 408.

4. Ibid., p. 409.

5. Edmund Asfour, "The Economic Framework of the Palestine Problem," in W. R. Polk, D. M. Stamier, and E. Asfour, *Backdrop to Tragedy* (Boston: Beacon Press, 1957), p. 311.

6. Robert Nathan, Oscar Gass, and Daniel Creamer, *Palestine: Problem and Promise* (Washington, D.C.: Public Affairs Press, 1946), p. 147

7. Gur Ofer, *The Service Industries in a Developing Economy: Israel as a Case Study* (New York: Frederick A. Praeger, 1967), p. 88.

8. Ibid.

9. Ibid., p. 114.

10. Ibid.

11. Ministry for Foreign Affairs, *Facts about Israel* (Jerusalem: Government Press, 1963), p. 46.

12. Nathan, Gass, and Creamer, *Palestine*, p. 224.

13. Esco Foundation for Palestine, *Palestine: A Study of Jewish, Arab, and British Policies*, vol.2 (New Haven: Yale University Press, 1947), p. 696.

14. Ibid., p. 697.

15. Ibid.

16. To protect themselves against cheap Arab competition, some Jews effected what amounted to a boycott of Arab production and expected their fellows to do the same.

17. Esco Foundation, *Palestine: A Study*, p. 729.

18. D. Horowitz and R. Hinden, *Economic Survey of Palestine* (Tel Aviv: Economic Research Institute, 1938), p. 118.

19. Ibid.

20. See Esco Foundation, *Palestine: A Study*, pp. 733-35.

21. Horowitz and Hinden, *Economic Survey*, p. 129.

22. Esco Foundation, *Palestine: A Study*, p. 1052.

23. E. Kleiman, "The Place of Manufacturing in the Growth of the Israel Economy," *Journal of Development Studies*, April 1967, p. 230.

24. Ibid.

25. Nathan, Gass, and Creamer, *Palestine*, p. 272.

26. Ibid., p. 278.

27. Horowitz and Hinden, *Economic Survey*, p. 134.

28. Esco Foundation, *Palestine: A Study*, p. 735.

29. Nathan, Gass, and Creamer, *Palestine*, p. 331-32.

30. Kleiman, "Israel Economy," p. 231.

31. Nathan, Gass, and Creamer, *Palestine*, p. 333.

32. Ibid., p. 335-36.

33. Robert Weigand, "The Arab League Boycott of Israel," *Business Topics*, Spring 1968, p. 76.

34. Ibid., p. 77.

35. Since its inception the League has grown in size, its present membership is Egypt, Jordan, Iraq, Syria, Lebanon, Libya, Tunisia, Sudan, Morrocco, Saudi Arabia, Yemen, Kuwait, and several Persian Gulf sheikdoms.

36. See Joseph Churba, "U.A.R.-Israel Rivalry over Aid and Trade in Saharan Africa: 1957-1963" (Ph.D. diss., Columbia University, 1965), particularly pp. 103-8.

37. Business International, *Coping with the Arab Boycott of Israel*, Management Monograph no. 19 (New York: Business International, 1963), p. 1. For a listing of eighteen offenses, most quite broadly defined, that result in blacklisting, see pp. 3-5.

38. See Susan Dworkin, "The Japanese and the Arab Boycott," *Near East Report*, October 1968, pp. 11-13; and "Japanese Firms Misread Arab Boycott Terms," *Business International*, 17 May 1968, p. 155.

39. See Losman, "International Economic Sanctions," pp. 231-33.

40. Ibid., pp. 238-41.

41. One Israeli official, commenting upon this statement is alleged to have quipped: "Of course it was an economic decision—there are 80 million thirsty Arabs and only a handful of Israelis."

42. Boutros-Ghali, "Arab League," p. 406.

43. See "Faisal Remark Stirs Up N.Y. Dinner Party," *Miami News,* 23 June 1966, p. 1.

44. "The Arab Boycott of Israel," *Business International,* 24 January 1964, p. 1.

45. "The Persistent Arab Boycott," *Business International,* 4 March 1966, p. 72. *Business Week,* 23 August 1969, p. 80, reported that the blacklist was "down to about 1,000 companies."

46. U.S., Department of Commerce, *Export Control, 83rd Quarterly Report* (Washington, D.C.: U.S. Government Printing Office, pp. 16-17.

47. U.S., Department of Commerce, *Export Control 87th Quarterly Report* (Washington, D.C.: U.S. Government Printing Office, 1969), p. 16.

48. U.S., Department of Commerce, *Export Control, 91st Quarterly Report* (Washington, D.C.: Government Printing Office, 1970), p. 15.

49. U.S., Congress, *Extending the Export Administration Act,* H. Rept. 94-1459, 94th Cong., 2d sess., September 1976, p. 43.

50. Harry B. Ellis, "The Arab-Israeli Conflict Today," in Georgiana G. Stevens, *The United States and the Middle East* (Englewood Cliffs, N.J.: Prenctice Hall, 1964), p. 132.

51. "How the Arab Boycott Works," *Business Abroad,* 17 April 1967, p. 22.

52. For a discussion of boycott loopholes, methods of contravening the embargo, and examples of smuggling, see Losman, "International Economic Sanctions," pp. 238-41.

53. It is probable that Jordan is the Arab country most seriously damaged by the boycott. Its loss of a direct route to the sea via the Haifa port and the failure to utilize jointly the Jordan waters constitute major direct impacts. The indirect costs in terms of other opportunities foregone are literally incalculable.

54. See Losman, "International Economic Sanctions," pp. 241-45, 383-86.

55. Quoted in "How the Arab Boycott Works," *Business Abroad,* 17 April 1967, p. 23.

56. "The Arab Boycott of Israel," *Business International,* 24 January 1964, p. 1.

57. Ellis, "The Arab-Israeli Conflict," p. 130.

58. Weigand, "Arab League Boycott," p. 75.

59. Marwan Iskandor, quoted in Imad Shehadeh, "Arab Boycott Hinders Israel," *Beirut Daily Star,* 7 May 1967.

60. Weigand, "Arab League Boycott," p. 80.

61. A. J. Meyer, *Middle Eastern Capitalism* (Cambridge, Mass.: Harvard University Press, 1959), p. 24.

62. Department of Economic and Social Affairs, *Ecomonic Developments in the Middle East, 1961-63* (New York: United Nations, 1965), pp. 76-78.

63. For a concise account of Israel's initial overtures and Arab counterpressures, see Rouhollah K. Ramazani, *The Middle East and the European Common Market* (Charlottesville: University Press of Virginia, 1964), pp. 70-74.

64. Finn B. Jensen and Ingo Walter, *The Common Market* (Philadelphia: J. B. Lippincott Company, 1965), pp. 123-24.

65. Modechai E. Kreinin, "Israel and the European Economic Community," *Quarterly Journal of Economics,* May 1968, pp. 297-312. Much progress with the EEC has since been made.

66. J. H. Thompson and R. D. Reischaucer, *Modernization of the Arab World* (Princeton: D. Van Nostrand Company, 1966), p. 74.

67. See Losman, "International Economic Sanctions," pp. 261-62.

68. Gardner Patterson, "Israel's Economic Problems," *Foreign Affairs,* January 1954, p. 321.

69. Harry B. Ellis, *Israel and the Middle East* (New York: Ronald Press Company, 1957), p. 162.

70. It can be argued that the existence of the boycott stimulated Israeli effort and ingenuity, which might not otherwise have been forthcoming. Such a hypothesis is not susceptible of empirical testing but is rejected nevertheless by this writer after a careful consideration of all the relevant data. If any stimulus exists, it probably derives more from the past armed conflicts and the constant threat of future ones. Finally, if it has existed, its duration and impact have probably been quite marginal and short-lived.

71. Mordehai Nahumi, "Policies and Practice of Occupation," *New Outlook,* May 1968, p. 32.

72. Walter Schwarz, "Israel's Bitter Honeymoon," *Manchester Guardian,* 8 May 1969, p. 7.

73. Economist Intelligence Unit, *Israel: Quarterly Economic Review* no. 4 (1968), p. 8.

74. Economist Intelligence Unit, *Israel: Quarterly Economic Review* no. 1 (1968), p. 7.

75. The inefficacy of boycott pressures in this regard is brought to the fore by the examples of air sabotage. Having failed in the purely economic sphere, other forms of warfare are being employed to bring an economic collapse.

76. A. Lerner and H. Ben-Shahar, *The Economies of Efficiency and Growth* (Cambridge, Mass.: Ballinger Publishing Company, 1975), p. 167.

77. "International Business," *Business Week,* 19 December 1977, p. 38.

78. "Arab League Boycott Chief Lashes Out at Egypt for Joint Venture with Ford," *Wall Street Journal,* 4 November 1977, p. 11.

79. See, for example, B'nai B'rith Current Issues Series, no. 197, *Arab Boycott* (Washington, D.C., n.d.), where the statement is made that the boycott "has not hampered Israel's economic growth."

Chapter 5

1. The terms "Rhodesia" and "Southern Rhodesia" will be used interchangeably. After the defeat of the Matabele armies (1895), two Rhodesias, one north and one south, were formally established. Northern Rhodesia is now Zambia.

2. See speech of Herbert Bowden, British Information Service, *Policy Statements: Rhodesia,* 8 December 1966.

3. J. E. S. Fawcett, "Security Council Resolutions on Rhodesia," *British Year Book of International Law, 1965-66,* eds. Waldock and Jennings (London: Royal Institute of International Affairs, 1968), p. 102.

4. Margery Perham, "The Rhodesian Crisis: Background," *International Affairs,* January 1966, p. 2.

5. Great Britain, *Memorandum of Native Policy in East Africa,* Cmd. 3573 (London: HMSO, 1930); and Great Britain, *Statement of the Conclusions as regards Close Union in East Africa,* Cmd. 3574 (London; HMSO, 1930).

6. Bowden, speech, *Policy Statements.*

7. Harm J. de Blij, *A Geography of Subsaharan Africa* (Chicago: Rand McNally & Co., 1964), p. 149.

8. Giovanni Arrighi, "The Political Economy of Rhodesia," *New Left Review,* September-October 1966, pp. 44-45.

9. Ibid., p. 45.

10. Ibid., pp. 46-57.

11. Timothy Curtin and David Murray, *Economic Sanctions and Rhodesia* (London: Insitute of Economic Affairs, 1967), p. 14.

12. "Non-African" is probably a more appropriate term than "white" because in additon to Europeans, there are a small number of Asians and other non-African groups generally identified statistically with the European element.

13. D. S. Pearson, "Employment Trends in a Developing Economy: The Case of Southern Rhodesia," *East African Economics Review*, June 1964, pp. 72-73.

14. Herbert J. Spiro, "The Rhodesias and Nyasaland," in *Five African States*, ed. Gwendolen Carter (Ithaca, N.Y.: Cornell University Press, 1963), p. 387.

15. Robert B. Sutcliffe, *Sanctions Against Rhodesia* (London: African Bureau, 1966).

16. Ibid., p. 4.

17. H. C. P. Anderson, *Rhodesia: A Field for Investment 1967* (Salisbury: H. C. P. Anderson, 1967), p. 29.

18. Perham, "Rhodesian Crisis," p. 7.

19. Ibid., pp. 7-8.

20. Heinz Portmann, "Rhodesia's Economy Under the Sanctions," *Swiss Review of World Affairs*, April 1967, p. 8.

21. Ibid.

22. Economist Intelligence Unit, *Rhodesia, Zambia, Malawi: Quarterly Economic Review Annual Supplement 1968*, p. 16.

23. Ibid.

24. Methods of avoidance are apparently limitless. Often Malawian export papers are attached to shipments. These are easily obtainable since the official Malawian documents were once printed in Salisbury. Certificates of origin from Mozambique, also readily obtainable, involve a similar deception. Indeed, use of false documents has become so common that often little care is taken to avoid detection, as when Rhodesian corned beef was mistakenly given a Mozambique certificate of origin rather than a Malawian (Mozambique does not produce corned beef).

25. Mauriel Horrel, *Days of Crisis in Rhodesia*, Fact Paper no. 16 (South African Institute of Race Relations, 1965), p. 43.

26. Frank Kearns, "A Report from Salisbury," telecast on CBS Evening News with Walter Cronkite, 21 March 1966 (reprinted in *African Report*, April 1966, p. 24).

27. B. Cockram, "Rhodesia—After the Tiger," address at Jan Smuts House, University of Witwatersrand, Johannesburg, 6 March 1967.

28. A. M. Hawkins, "The Rhodesian Economy under Sanctions," *Rhodesian Journal of Economics*, August 1967, p. 51

29. A. M. Hawkins, "Rhodesian Economy under Siege," *Bulletin of the Africa Institute of South Africa* 1 (1975), p. 15

30. It is of interest that official Rhodesian statistics are somewhat at variance, as noted in the Ministry of Finance, *Economic Survey of Rhodesia* (Salisbury: Government Printer, 1967, 1968, 1969). The 1967 *Economic Survey* shows capital inflows as roughly equivalent to the current account shortfall. The 1968 *Economic Survey* shows 1967 capital inflows to have been 35 percent higher than the current account deficit, while the 1969 *Economic Survey* shows the 1967 inflows to be 75.6 percent greater! Revisions in such data, however, are not infrequent and are found in U.S. statistics as well. See Fritz Machlup *International Payments, Debts, and Gold* (New York: Charles Scribner's Sons, 1964), chap.7.

31. Sales of pig iron to Mexico and Peru were reported at one-half the world price. Sales to Japan were also reported. See Arthur Bottomley, "Rhodesia: Effect of Sanctions," speech at Commonwealth Parliamentary Conference, Montreal, 30 September 1966, printed 4 October 1966, by British Information Services, *Policy Statements*.

32. Hawkins, "Rhodesian Economy under Siege," p. 15.

33. *Economic Survey of Rhodesia 1975*, p. 8.

34. Neil McInnes, "The World at Work," *Barron's*, 15 June 1975, p. 29.

35. "Rhodesia," *Commonwealth Survey*, 7 January 1966, p. 17.

36. Hawkins, "The Rhodesian Economy under Sanctions," p. 52.

37. Portmann, "Rhodesia's Economy," pp. 11-12.

38. "Rhodesian Tobacco," *Financial Mail*, 16 May 1975.

39. Economist Intelligence Unit, *Rhodesia, Zambia, Malawi: Quarterly Economic Review Annual Supplement 1968*, p. 7.

40. Economist Intelligence Unit, *Rhodesia, Zambia, Malawi: Quarterly Economic Review* 2 (1969), p. 8.

41. "Rhodesia," *Standard Bank Review*, August 1968, p. 16.

42. Lee Kanner, *World Economic Review and Forecast: 1967* (New York: Grosset and Dunlop, 1967), p. 237.

43. "Rhodesia," *Europa Yearbook 1974*, vol. 2 (London: Europa Publications Limited, 1974, p. 1271.

44. Ibid.

45. R. B. Sutcliffe, "Stagnation and Inequality in Rhodesia 1946–1968," *Bulletin of the Africa Institute of South Africa*, February 1971, p. 36.

46. Hawkins, "Rhodesian Economy Under Seige," p. 15.

47. Ibid.

48. Hawkins, "The Rhodesian Economy Under Sanctions," p. 47.

49. *Europa Yearbook 1974*, p. 1273.

50. Economist Intelligence Unit, *Rhodesia, Zambia, Malawi: Quarterly Economic Review Annual Supplement 1968*, p. 11.

51. Ibid.

52. Ibid., p. 10.

53. *Europa Yearbook 1974*, p. 1275.

54. Curtin and Murray, *Economic Sanctions and Rhodesia*, passim.

55. *Economic Survey of Rhodesia, 1975*, p. 13.

56. Hawkins, "The Rhodesian Economy Under Sanctions," p. 48.

57. Ibid.

58. Economist Intelligence Unit, *Rhodesia, Zambia, Malawi: Quarterly Economic Review Annual Supplement 1968*, p. 4.

59. Economist Intelligence Unit, *Rhodesia, Zambia, Malawi: Quarterly Ecomonic Review* 2 (1969), p. 7.

60. *Economic Survey of Rhodesia, 1975*, p. 21.

61. Svetozar Pejovich, "Some Important Factors in the Economic Growth of Rhodesia," *South African Journal of Economics*, June 1970, p. 140.

62. Hawkins, "Rhodesian Economy Under Siege," p. 13.

63. Ibid.

64. Hawkins, "The Rhodesian Economy Under Sanctions," p. 46.

65. T. Curtin, "Sanctions and Rhodesia: A Reply to R. T. McKinnel," *African Affairs*, January 1969, p. 57. See also *Economic Survey of Rhodesia 1966*, tables 3 and 19.

66. Quoted in "Farm Wages," *Financial Mail*, 30 May 1973, p. 818.

67. Sutcliff, "Stagnation and Inequality in Rhodesia," p. 40.

68. "A Lesson to Learn," *Financial Mail*, 14 December 1973, p. 110.

69. *Economic Survey of Rhodesia, 1975*, p. 23.

70. W. H. Hutt, to author, 3 December 1975.

71. *Economic Survey of Rhodesia, 1972, 1975*, pp. 21, 20.

72. In early 1977 income taxes were increased 10 percent and sales taxes increased 50 percent. These measures were designed to raise an extra $35 million to meet the rising costs of increased military actions.

73. U.S. Department of State, Bureau of Public Affairs, *The Secretary of State: Statement, 13 May 1976* (Washington, D.C.: Government Printing Office), p. 4.

74. "World-Wide," *Wall Street Journal*, 9 March 1978, p. 1.

Chapter 6

1. Leonard Kapungu, *The United Nations and Economic Sanctions Against Rhodesia* (Lexington, Mass.: Lexington Books, 1975), p. 53.

2. John Galtung, "On the Effects of International Economic Sanctions," *World Politics,* April 1967, p. 390.

3. Ibid., p. 392.

4. Paul Scott, "Red Menace in Africa," *Monroe (La.) Morning World,* 28 December 1977, p. 4A.

5. Richard R. Leger, "Secret Trade Illustrates South Africa's Power," *Wall Street Journal,* 9 December 1977, p. 25.

6. Kapungu, *U.N. and Economic Sanctions,* p. 129.

7. David Grumpert, "Yankee Businessmen Get a VIP Welcome," *Wall Street Journal,* 30 November 1977, p. 33.

8. President Carter's own faith in the efficacy of sanctions may be indicated by his shelving a suggestion to get Latin American and Western European governments to agree to reduce their Cuban trade until Castro withdraws some of his troops from Angola. See Scott, "Red Menace in Africa," p. 4A.

9. In March 1977, at the urging of President Carter and the State Department, the Byrd Amendment, which had softened U.S. compliance with U.N. sanctions by allowing American imports of Rhodesian chrome, was repealed. It has since been reported that with the rising price of metallurgical chrome, the State Department has done an about face and suggested that the U.S. Treasury ignore the enforcement of the restored embargo! Senator Byrd has also noted that Great Britain vigorously protested the repeal of the Byrd Amendment "because she has to certify that her steel products coming to this country contain no Rhodesian chrome." See Robert S. Allen, "Chrome Situation Turns to Lead," *Monroe (La.) Morning World,* 28 May 1977, p. 4A.

10. S. Synnestvedt, "Red Drive in Cuba," *Current History,* October 1963, p. 242.

Selected Bibliography

Boorstein, Edward. *The Economic Transformation of Cuba.* New York: Monthly Review Press, 1968.

Clark, Evans, ed. *Boycotts and Peace: Report by the Committee on Economic Sanctions.* New York: Harper and Brothers, 1932.

Cuban Economic Research Project. *A Study on Cuba.* Miami: University of Miami Press, 1965.

Curtin, Timothy R. "Rhodesian Economic Development under Sanctions and 'The Long Haul,'" *African Affairs,* April 1968, pp. 101-10.

————, and Murray, David. *Economic Sanctions and Rhodesia.* London: Institute of Economic Affairs, 1967.

Dagan, A. "The Arab Boycott." In *The Israel Year Book 1966,* edited by L. Berger, pp. 252-54. Jerusalem: Israel Yearbook Publications, 1966.

De Crespigny, A. R. C., and McKinnell, R. T. "The Nature and Significance of Economic Boycott." *South African Journal of Economics,* December 1960, pp. 319-36.

Doxey, Margaret P. *Economic Sanctions and International Enforcement.* New York: Oxford University Press, 1971.

Feis, Herbert. *Three International Episodes: Seen from E.A.* New York: W. W. Norton and Company, 1966.

Galtung, John. "On the Effects of International Economic Sanctions." *World Politics,* April 1967, pp. 378-416.

Guevara, Ernesto Che. "The Cuban Economy." *International Affairs,* October 1964, pp. 589-99.

Hawkins, A. M. "The Rhodesian Economy under Sanctions." *Rhodesian Journal of Economics,* August 1967, pp. 44-60.

————. "Rhodesian Economy under Siege." *Bulletin of the Africa Institute of South Africa,* no. 1 (1975), pp. 12-18, 23.

Horowitz, David. *The Economics of Israel.* New York: Pergamon Press, 1967.

Kapungu, Leonard. *The United Nations and Economic Sanctions Against Rhodesia.* Lexington, Mass.: Lexington Books, 1975.

Kearns, Frank. "A Report from Salisbury." Telecast on CBS Evening News with Walter Cronkite, 21 March 1966. Reprinted in *Africa Report,* April 1966.

Kemp, Murray. "The Gain from International Trade." *Economic Journal,* December 1962, pp. 803-19.

Kindleberger, Charles P. *Foreign Trade and the National Economy.* New Haven: Yale University Press, 1962.

Kleiman, Eli. "The Place of Manufacturing in the Growth of the Israel Economy." *Journal of Development Studies,* April 1967, pp. 226-48.

Kreinin, Mordechai, E. "Israel and the European Economic Community." *Quarterly Journal of Economics,* May 1968, pp. 297-312.

Linneman, H. *An Econometric Study of International Trade Flows.* Amsterdam: North Holland Publishing Company, 1966.

Losman, Donald. "The Economics of Bloc Aid and Trade with Cuba." *Marquette Business Review,* Summer 1970, pp. 68-77.

Nahumi, Mordehai. "Policies and Practice of Occupation." *New Outlook,* May 1968, pp. 26-42.

Patterson, Gardner. "Israel's Economic Problems." *Foreign Affairs,* January 1954, pp. 310-22.

Remer, Charles F. *A Study of Chinese Boycotts.* Baltimore: John Hopkins Press, 1933.

Segal, Ronald. *Sanctions Against South Africa.* Baltimore: Penguin Books, 1964.

Sutcliffe, Robert B. *Sanctions Against Rhodesia.* London: African Bureau, 1966.

Turck, Nancy. "The Arab Boycott of Israel." *Foreign Affairs,* April 1977, pp. 472-493.

U.S., Department of Commerce. *Export Control, 83rd Quarterly Report.* Washington, D.C.: Government Printing Office, 1968.

Weigand, Robert. "The Arab Boycott of Israel." *Business Topics,* Spring 1968, pp. 74-80.

Wilkins, John R. "Legal Norms and International Economic Development: The Case of the Cuba Shipping Restriction in the United States Foreign Assistance Act." *California Law Review,* October 1967, pp. 977-1019.

Index

access to markets, and benefits of trade, 8–9
Albania, sanctions against, 5–6
Alexandria Protocol of 1944, 60
Arab League, 47–49, 57–62. *See also* Israel, Arab boycott of
Argentina, trade with Cuba of, 45
Arrighi, Giovanni, 87

Beira, blockade of, 79
blacklisting, by Arab League, 57–62
BMC, 109–10
Boorstein, Edward, 30–31
Bowden, Herbert, 82
Boycott, Captain Charles, 3
boycott, etymology of, 2–3
boycotts: in American colonies, 2; disadvantages of, 3–4; economic effectiveness of, 1; and humanitarianism, 3–4; multilateral, 2; political effectiveness of, 1; purpose of, 1; unilateral, 2; universal, 2. *See also* economic sanctions
Byrd amendment, 122, 136–37

Castro, Fidel, 21
Central Boycott Office, 49, 57–62. *See also* Israel, Arab boycott of
Céspedes, Manuel, 28
China: boycotts by, 2; trade with Cuba of, 28, 41
Coca-Cola, 39–40, 59, 64, 78
comparative costs, differences in, 7–8
Council on Mutual Economic Aid, 5. *See also* Soviet bloc
Cuba: dependence on Soviet bloc of, 43; exchange controls in, 27; foreign policy of, 44, 131; growth rates of, 37, 43; import dependence of, 30–31; import substitution in, 18, 38–39, 43; investment capacity of, 36–38; O.A.S. sanctions against, 5, 21, 43–45, 134; petroleum conservation in, 39; petroleum imports of, 27–28; prerevolutionary foreign trade of, 22–23; postrevolutionary trading partners of, 23–25; rationing in, 41–42; rice imports of, 28, 41; spare parts problems of, 32–35; sugar industry of, 12, 13–14, 26, 34–35; tourist industry of, 12, 14, 42, 44; trade with China

of, 28, 41; trade with Soviet block of, 13, 15–16, 22–28, 31–32, 39, 41, 42; trade with United States of, 20–21, 22; transportation industry of, 34; warehousing problems of, 36
Cuba, U.S. boycott of: and balance of payments, 26–27; capital effects of, 36–38; and capital stock, 42; and consumption patterns, 40–42, 43; contravention of, 29–30; and domestic economizing, 39; effectiveness of, 45–46; and growth of output, 43; and hard-currency earnings, 24, 26, 28; and import substitution, 38–39; indirect costs of, 13; other nations' noncompliance with, 43–45; political effects of, 128–29, 130; and quality of goods, 39–40; relaxation of, 44, 45, 134; technological impact of, 32–36; and terms of trade, 42; and transport costs, 12, 27–28
Cuban revolution, 20–21

"demonstration effect," 9
division of labor, and benefits of trade, 8, 9
Dominican Republic, sanctions against, 5

economic sanctions: capital effects of, 11, 13–14; as collusive arrangement, 136–37; conditions for effectiveness of, 125–26, 128, 132–34; contravention of, 126, 136–37; costs of, to boycotting states, 14, 137; deined, 1, 124; direct costs of, 11–12; economic effects of, 10–16; effectiveness of, 15–16, 17–19; and emigration, 134–36; enforcement of, 133, 138–39; evaluation of, 16–18; failure of, 124, 125, 136; and import substitution, 126–27; indirect costs of, 12–13; partial, 2, 126; political effects of, 130; and public opinion, 131–32; and restructuring of trade patterns, 127; and self-sacrifice, 128; theory of, 124–25; and third-party states, 137–38, 139; unpredictable impact of, 127–28. *See also* boycotts; embargoes
Ecuador Sugar Mill, 35
efficiency, and trade, 9
Egypt, and Arab boycott of Israel, 78–79
elasticity of import demand, 15–16